William Coltman VC

The Story of
Two Crosses

William Coltman VC

The Story of
Two Crosses

by

Anthony Tideswell

Decapolis Press Publications

First edition printed by: Sovereign Book Care, Stoke-on-Trent, 2008

Printed in the UK

Contents

Foreword

This is the story of two crosses. It is not a history of the Great War on the Western front nor is it a biography of a very brave man. William Harold Coltman was the most decorated non-commissioned officer of that terrible conflict. Besides winning the Victoria Cross for gallantry, he was also awarded four other medals for bravery and mentioned in dispatches during just over three years of service in the trenches of Northern France. Yet he never fired a shot in anger!

In May 2008 I stood at the foot of the grave of Noel Chavasse VC and bar, the only man to win the highest award for gallantry twice during the First World War. Like Bill Coltman he never used a weapon against another man during his time on the Somme and near Ypres where he was to die tragically, succumbing to multiple wounds. Yet the differences between the two men were great. Chavasse was born into a middle class background; his father was the Bishop of Liverpool. Coltman had no such upbringing. Leaving school at thirteen he looked to labouring on the land for the modest lifestyle he enjoyed throughout his life.

Looking at the two crosses engraved on Chavasse's grave, my thoughts turned to the two crosses which were a feature of Bill Coltman's life. Here was yet another similarity: saving the lives of comrades in winning the second VC had cost Noel his life. In importance the Victoria Cross which Bill Coltman won in 1918 was of no value compared to the cross which had been central to his whole life – the cross of Calvary. This cross had led his Saviour to die, the death of the Son of God had been the price paid to save millions like Bill. Whatever Coltman VC had risked to save his comrades from death paled into insignificance when he considered that which his Saviour had given for him almost two thousand years ago.

My introduction to the amazing story of this most brave Christian man came almost seventeen years ago when one of his grandchildren, John, was speaking to a group in a local residential home. An invitation to attend the opening of Coltman House in Burton had coincided with the marriage of one of John's sons. He used this to illustrate the relationship between a father and son – between the Father and the Son. Afterwards I asked John why the Duke of York had come to open a building bearing William Coltman's name. I realized that although I had enjoyed a long interest in the Great War I had never heard of this man. Why was this?

The answer was that for this most gallant of men that which he had done was part of the past. His avoidance of interviews and publicity has led to few knowing very much about a very remarkable soldier. Perhaps this short account will help to remedy this and enable others to enjoy the Christian certainty which he had in abundant measure.

For me the research, collating and writing of this account has been an exercise in being able to find out just enough from family, friends and unit records to be able to state, categorically, that William Coltman VC, DCM and Bar, MM and Bar is one of the most gallant and least recognized heroes of the First World War. Yet he would have been the last man to have regarded himself as a hero. His lack of interviews was indicative of his wider reaction to the conflict which had brought him temporary fame and military honour. For him, those days belonged to the past. As a deeply devout Christian man he looked to the present and the future with the same degree of certainty with which he consigned the past to memory. His gallant and untiring service to others, friend and foe alike, had been carried out with the saving of life as his aim. In his life before and after the period from 1915 to 1918 Bill Coltman was more concerned with the spiritual, eternal nature of life as he recognized it. He was no fool; the fool says that there is no God and heads for certain destruction whereas foremost in Bill's life was devotion to and service for God.

The debt which he owed to his Lord for his salvation would be worked out in his commitment to the lives of others. His care for the eternal well-being of those around him would be temporarily supplemented by his care for the earthly life of his fellow men in the trenches of France. That he would carry out these tasks with a recurring devotion to duty which staggers us today, would be the logical approach by a man who would do so for his God and his fellow man. The demands of the two were indivisibly linked. In saving the lives of countless victims of war, he would merely reflect the devotion and sacrifice which had led Christ to the cross. All that he did would be to save others, looking to 'the author and finisher of faith' to direct him.

When, and if you finish this account, you will marvel at how this man survived the ordeal of the Western Front. When the average life expectancy for a front-line soldier was between twenty and thirty minutes during an attack, it can only be assumed this man was truly protected by the hand of God during his countless forays into 'No Man's Land'. Bill Coltman would be more hopeful, if alive, that you would marvel at how his Saviour had given all He had to die for him and countless others. Truly this is a record of salvation, earthly and heavenly.

Preface to the Second Edition

I am indebted to the Coltman family who initiated this project and who have worked tirelessly to promote this account of a truly remarkable man.

The first edition sold out quickly and raised almost £1000 for Armed Services' charities.

The support of the National Arboretum, near Lichfield, and Coltman House in supporting this has been much appreciated.

May I add that the surprising success of this book has been due solely to the remarkable man who is the central character of it and the nature of his devotion to his Lord and his fellow man.

Anthony Tideswell
February 2016

John's memories of his Grandad

William Harold Coltman was a quiet unassuming family man. He had two children and four grandchildren. Prior to going into the army, he was a gardener and, when he returned, he continued in this role.

He worked for the Burton Corporation and, latterly, looked after a recreation ground which could be seen from his living room window. He also tended an area nearby which had a number of flower beds, known throughout the area for their beauty. He had a love of flowers and provided the plants himself. He had a number of allotments which provided vegetables throughout the year.

The reason why William Harold Coltman would not take up arms during his time in the army was because of his Christian beliefs. All of his adult life he was involved with an independent group of Christians who regularly met in the meeting room in the heart of the village of Winshill.

In his early days he was jointly responsible for the Sunday school, where many village children came. He also, with other members of the group, would provide financially and in a practical way for the upkeep of the building. It was from there that his military funeral took place. It was full to capacity with family, friends and army personnel and many others listening outside.

Much of the recognition of his brave exploits has arisen since his death. Maybe this is what he would have wanted because we never remember him ever discussing any of his war time experiences.

Acknowledgements

The impetus for this book came from discussions with John Coltman, Bill's grandson. John has provided his time and assistance in the development of this project for which I am very appreciative.

The Coltman family has been a great help in seeking out information about a very elusive figure who was not known for his verbosity! My thanks to David, Jackie, Barbara, Linda and Marion for their kind assistance, hospitality and material provided.

The staff at the Staffordshire Regimental Museum at Whittington Barracks provided material and assistance for which I am very thankful. The 1/6th Battalion War Diary was a primary source of great interest and information. My visit also confirmed their great respect for Bill Coltman which is exemplified in the naming of their trench display.

Captain Pat Forrest MBE, senior officer at Coltman House, Burton, also allowed access to the portrait and other artefacts displayed there as well as providing some interesting and valuable observations.

Chapter One

'The day of one's birth',
Ecclesiastes chapter 7 verse 1

William Harold Coltman was born on the 17th of November 1891 in the little village of Rangemore near Burton-on-Trent, Staffordshire. His father, Charles Coltman was a gardener at Tatenhill Common and the family lived in a tied-cottage belonging to the estate of Lord Burton. The cottage stands there today, just along from the small school which William first attended in 1894. He was one of five brothers and they all attended the local school. Visiting Rangemore today, little seems to have changed in over a century. The cottage still stands, built in 1818, one of three instead of the original four. Modern cars travel along the road which once was host to the horses and carts which journeyed through the village. The school is modernized and yet the main assembly hall has changed little in the intervening time. Now a framed photograph of its most famous pupil looks down on the children; the teachers of 1894 would have been surprised if they knew that, over a hundred years later, young William Coltman's picture would be hanging there.

Certainly, there was nothing to make the boy stand out during his ten years at the school. Unlike his siblings, the school logbooks for that period have no mention of him, suggesting that his reputation for mischievousness, if true, was gained later in his life. When he left school there were no obvious signs of it.

William's father died while he was at school. Times must have been hard for a widow trying to raise five children in an agricultural environment. Annie Coltman looked for work to support her young family and Bill, like the others, would help to deliver fresh milk, travelling around the area on a horse and trap. It was a healthy lifestyle for the youngster and probably meant that he grew up fitter and healthier than his urban-dwelling contemporaries.

In 1904 William left school and found work to help the family. For a young man from a rural background it was quite natural to seek employment in the footsteps of his late father and so William moved to Duffield in Derbyshire to seek work on the land for a time. Later, he became gardener to Colonel C. J. Goer at Bleak House. This prompted his move back to Burton where he lived at 60, Forest Road. Later in his life, after the Great War, he would return to employment with the Colonel.

While working at Repton as a gardener, William met the woman with whom he would share 35 years of happy marriage. Eleanor May Dolman was, like William, a devout Christian. They were married at Burton Register Office on January 8th 1913. This might seem strange to people today who might expect two committed Christians to marry in a church. However, Eleanor and William attended the Meeting of the 'Christian Brethren' in Winshill, which held its gatherings in, firstly, the farmhouse, and then the adjacent granary belonging to Mr Kent in Hawfield Lane. This building would not have been licensed, or been appropriate for weddings.

The 'Brethren' Meeting at Winshill had been founded about ten years before. For the nonconformist churches, including those belonging to the so-called 'Christian Brethren' this was a time of expansion and outreach, particularly among the working-class areas of England. This was still an age of Edwardian certainty when 'God ruled overall and Britain ruled over a quarter of the World's population'. Children at school would learn 'scripture' daily and be reminded of how much 'pink' there was on the World Map at the back of the classroom. Today, it is difficult for us to understand that age – it was shaken by the massive conflagration which would commence in 1914; it disappeared in the years which followed on from 1945. For William and Eleanor there would be a short period of this era to enjoy; blessed by their first child, a son, born later in the year and appropriately named after his late grandfather, Charles.

For William Coltman, his belonging to the 'Brethren' was a life-defining factor throughout his eighty-three years. He would attend regularly until his death, serving as an overseer in his latter years. However, William would never have said that he belonged to any church. He would have claimed to belong to His Saviour, the Lord Jesus Christ. His conversion, whenever it took place, would be the turning point. From that moment he would have believed that every part of his life would be under the guidance of God – that God's will would be done in all things, whether in his home, marriage, or, later, the trenches of Northern France.

At this point, it is necessary to digress from our narrative to provide an outline of the 'Brethren'. Without some understanding of their beliefs and practices it would be impossible to understand the reasoning which caused Bill Coltman to act in the manner he did from 1916 to 1918 and to appreciate his reaction to the awards which were granted to him for his actions.

The Plymouth Brethren is a title used to describe, not wholly accurately, a nonconformist Christian movement that grew out of the late eighteenth and nineteenth century, alongside other groups such as the Methodist Connexion and The Needed Truth. Finding their roots in the area of Plymouth, this geographical epithet has remained, although now meaningless and not used by the members of the fellowships today. The early 'Brethren' emphasized the doctrine of salvation by God's grace rather than good works, 'the priesthood of all believers' giving rise to a totally lay ministry, and the complete autonomy of each group or meeting. From this arose a strong belief in the predetermined nature of God's involvement in the life of the individual believer. The 'Brethren' movement divided into two distinct groups, mainly due to a difference in interpretation over 'separation' and church government. To explain: some 'Brethren' believed in a centralized form of Church government where matters of practice were decided centrally; others believed that each company or 'meeting' was responsible for its own decisions and was not answerable to a centralized governing body. The most 'centralist' groups separated to form what is known as the 'Exclusive Brethren'; the most independent and most numerous became known as the 'Open' or 'Christian Brethren'.

William Coltman belonged to the 'Christian Brethren' and met with his fellow believers in Winshill. By now he was living with his family nearby and was active in Sunday School work, Bible study and the Gospel meetings which were a feature of each Sunday or 'Lord's Day' as it would have been referred to then. It is hard for us to appreciate what a Sunday would have been like for people in the far-off days of 1913. For those, like Bill, living on the land it would have been the regular 'day of rest'. Strict in his beliefs, he would have done no work; not even milk would have been delivered to the home. The Sunday routine would have began with the family, dressed in sober and modest clothing of the best quality affordable, setting off in the morning for the 'Breaking of Bread'. Gathering around a simple table with the communion emblems of bread and wine upon it, the meeting would consist of hymn singing, audible prayer from the men present, Bible reading and exposition. There would be no set format, all brethren would lead the worship as led by the Holy Spirit, singing being unaccompanied by any musical instrument. At some point, brethren would give thanks for the loaf and the cup of wine and it would be passed round the group, all who belonged to the fellowship partaking. A bag or box would be passed around for the offering. Later in the day Sunday school would be held, Bill having a class of boys to teach, concentrating on the Bible and the demands of good, honest Christian living. This would have been emphasized again in the evening Gospel Service, when one of the brethren from Winshill, or from a nearby meeting, would be responsible for the preaching. Not all brethren took part in the gospel preaching. Throughout his life, Bill did so on only rare occasions, but would offer his testimony of how he became a Christian and take part in the open air gatherings which were convened from time to time in the streets adjacent to the Meeting House.

It is important to appreciate this aspect of Bill Coltman's life because it infused his very being. Living for and following the teachings of God in the Bible became the *raison d'etre* for Bill's existence on earth. He was placed here 'for a season' to love God and his fellow men. These were the direct commands of his Lord and Saviour as recorded in Matthew's Gospel chapters 19 and 20. More than this, in whatever circumstances or perils he found himself, he firmly believed that God would always retain overall control of his life. In the 'shadow of death' God would be alongside. Like all brethren, Bill would have read the Bible daily and taken to heart what it says. Consider the words of the Book of Deuteronomy Chapter 32 in the light of the upheavals which were to change Bill's life before his twenty-fifth birthday:

'In a desert land he found him, in a barren and howling waste. He shielded him and cared for him; he guarded him as the apple of his eye, like an eagle that stirs up its nest and hovers over its young, that spreads its wing to catch them and carries them on its pinions. The Lord alone led him; no foreign god was with him'.[1]

We can all read these words today for ourselves. It is one thing to read them; Bill Coltman believed them. The word of God would be the arbiter in all decisions he took as a father, a husband, a soldier and as a man. It was not simply his decision; whatever personal views he had, they must always be 'tested' by scriptural truth and only be acted upon when certain that God would be honoured. No details of how or when Bill became a Christian exist today; what we know is that it occurred at some point prior to his marriage and that it changed his life ever after.

---

[1] Deuteronomy chapter 32 verse 10. Quoted from the New International Version, International Bible Society, 1973.

Chapter Two

'A noise of war in the camp',
Exodus chapter 32 verse 17

The summer of 1914 was one of the warmest and sunniest of the twentieth century. For a family like the Coltmans it would have been filled with the vital elements of any other summer for those working on the land. Bill would have been very aware of the changing seasons – the need to plough and prepare, to seed and to tend and then to wait on God's provision in the sun and rain which would determine the quality and quantity of the harvest. A good harvest would mean more plentiful and cheaper fruit and vegetables; for the poorer in society, and those working on the land in particular, this could mean the difference between comfort and suffering. The country skills of jam making and food preservation would have been to the fore and in August, as the early harvests appeared, eyes would be fixed on the fields and bushes rather than on the town of Sarajevo in the far off Balkans. With modern satellite communications we are used to instant news – we can be aware, and see pictures of, a tsunami or terrorist atrocity within minutes of the event taking place. It is unlikely that the Coltmans would have even heard of Sarajevo, never mind realize that the assassination of the Archduke Ferdinand of Austria and his wife in the previous month would set off a series of events which would plunge Europe into the most catastrophic war ever seen, the costliest in lives for Britain in its history.

Britain's declaration of war on August 4th was a surprise. Even many members of Parliament, whose focus had been on the Irish situation, were stunned by the pace of events which had led to mobilization by Russia, Austria, Germany and France, closely followed by Great Britain and her Empire. The detail of the mechanisms which sent Europe to war are outside the scope of this account. Suffice to state that since her defeat in the Franco-Prussian war of 1870, followed by the subsequent crowning of the first German Emperor at

Versailles, France had viewed the developing industrial might of a united Germany with alarm. The 'new Germany', with a rapidly expanding population of nearly 60 million, saw itself as the leading economic and military power in Europe, a role previously held by their western neighbour. Britain's eyes had been firmly fixed on her great worldwide Empire. Her navy was viewed as being all important as it safeguarded economic wealth by protecting trade routes to other countries. Central European disputes had little effect on the British outlook; traditionally, the sea power or 'gunboat diplomacy' of the nineteenth century had been sufficient. However, the developing power of Germany had caused some British statesmen to focus a little more on this area. Far thinking politicians such as Haldane had realized that the 'balance of power' was shifting to this 'new kid on the block'. The traditional enemy, France, had lost prestige, besides the territories of Alsace and Lorraine in the 1870 war. When Kaiser Wilhelm II became emperor and dismissed his trusted chancellor Otto von Bismarck, it marked a new, more aggressive development in German foreign policy. The subsequent development of the Kiel Canal to allow German warships to enter the North Sea was combined with a rapid increase in warship building. These events caused France to seek a mutual alliance or *entente* as the established powers sought to protect their interests. However, it was the French alliance with Russia which led directly to conflict, as the Russians mobilized their forces to prevent Austria invading Serbia. As a consequence of the events in Sarajevo, the five leading powers of Europe found themselves drawn inexorably into war. Before too long, millions of French, Russian, German, Austrian and British servicemen would be dead – the shooting of an Austrian Archduke had provided a 'spark' which ignited all the national distrust and racial hatred which had smouldered for so long.

Britain could not tolerate a German invasion of the Channel ports along the Belgian and French coastline. Strategically, it had to be prevented by diplomacy, or stopped by military action. When Germany failed to give assurances about observing Belgian neutrality, the British cabinet had little option but to join their

French and Russian allies in going to war. Within days of the declaration, the first elements of Britain's army were embarking for Northern France. Now, however, the harvest of Britain's neglect of the strategic importance of her army began to become apparent. Britain was prepared for war in some respects – recent reforms had led to well-trained and equipped forces. The war book, the brainchild of a General Douglas Haig among others, meant that the British Expeditionary Force (BEF) under the command of Sir John French moved efficiently from its bases in Britain, transported by the ubiquitous navy across the Channel to centre on the area around Mauberge. The great difficulty was not the quality but the quantity of the British forces. A force consisting of less than 160,000 men was not large enough to impact decisively on an enemy force approaching four million, nearly half of which were bearing down on Belgium in a swinging hook to envelope Paris from the north and end the war in six weeks. It was elements of this mighty force which the BEF met near the little town of Mons in their first engagement and, despite causing some casualties by their excellence in rifle fire, the BEF was forced to retire from the field, overwhelmed by sheer numbers. The hasty and long retreat which followed to the outskirts of Paris exhausted the small British force, which lost nearly a quarter of its original number in less than a month.

While many at home believed that the war would be over soon, some leading figures, like Lord Kitchener, the famous Field Marshall who was now Minister for War, realized that it would last far longer. Kitchener envisaged an army of over three million and a war lasting as long as four years. Many thought him insane, but his predictions were to be underestimates. By 1918 over five million men would be in uniform, and the war would last for nearly four and a half years, changing this country forever. Kitchener's call for volunteers to form a new army galvanized the British public in the aftermath of the battles at Mons and Le Cateau. Although the initial call had been for 100,000 volunteers, by the end of the year over a million men had enlisted to fight.

No one knows what Bill Coltman's initial reaction was to these events. He was a committed Christian, married for less than two years and with responsibilities as a parent and provider. The first months of the war coincided with harvest time, always extremely important for those on the land. How well informed he would have been about the events in Belgium and France it is hard to say. As a member of a group which sought to live by the word of God (the Bible) rather than be influenced by politics and politicians, more pressing matters in family, spiritual and work life may have taken up his thoughts. It is a fact that, even today, most of the adults belonging to the 'Brethren' choose not to vote; some assiduously avoid anything to do with the media, not owning televisions or even radios. I remember being told personally by a member that he had not known for 48 hours about the announcement of the end of the war in Europe in May, 1945. He had no access to radio or newspapers.

The issues that concerned Bill Coltman throughout the rest of 1914 are unknown to us today. He has left no record of them with his family or friends. One can assume that he would be conversant with the news that dominated that period but details of the conduct of the war would be few. After a period when censorship at the front had been minimal, during the retreat from Mons and the advances following the pivotal battle on the Marne, news from the front was strictly censored and the press carried 'tales of daring' rather than a balanced appreciation of the role of the BEF. Statistics show that the initial summer appeal for recruits was not followed by an uncontrollable rush to the recruiting centres. Most chose to wait and see what might happen; when news of casualties in the early BEF battles got back, a much greater number came forward.

By the first winter, the Western Front had settled into the pattern that was to dominate for the next three years. The withdrawing German army had chosen the 'best ground' on which to dig in, building trenches from the Channel coast to Switzerland which were remarkable for their sophistication. Although as 1915 approached these were nowhere near as comprehensive as they would become, the strategic failings of the United Kingdom Government became apparent. Kitchener had remarked that it was brave but rather foolhardy to declare war on the greatest army in the world when having fewer than 5% of their force. The more powerful French and Russian armies had squandered men and material in fruitless offensives although in the west the enemy had been halted and forced to retire and the Russian army had entered East Prussia for a short period.

Fundamentally for the British army, there was a lack of manpower and an even greater shortage of heavy artillery, ammunition and weapons suitable for the trench warfare that had developed. Even rifles were in short supply and soldiers had been forced to use the obsolete longer version of the Lee Enfield and the highly unreliable Canadian Ross rifles. In January 1915, as troops suffered the cold and privations of the front, William Harold Coltman presented himself at the recruiting office in Burton, and volunteered for the local Territorial Unit, the 6th Battalion of the North Staffordshire Regiment.

Chapter Three

'And departed into Egypt',
Matthew chapter 2 verse 14

Before we look at Bill Coltman's service in the ranks we should examine briefly the structure of the British army in 1915. Compared to the Royal Navy, the army had always been a neglected and relatively ignored branch of the armed forces. Unlike the Senior Service the army enjoyed no royal title – it still does not today! Indeed, the United Kingdom government is seeking ways to improve the national awareness of its current soldiers; it was little different in the nineteenth and early twentieth centuries. The Regular Army had been drastically reorganized in the aftermath of the Boer War. This conflict had illustrated the effect of years of stagnation and neglect by successive British governments. The previous Cardwell Reforms of 1881 had re-structured the Regulars on a local county basis and this had helped to develop a strong regimental tradition. It has also aligned the Regular Forces with the County Militia and Yeomanry who were designed to protect the homeland when and where required in an emergency. A Royal Commission in 1904 had reported that these local volunteer forces were entirely incapable of defending Britain and so Lord Haldane, assisted by leading army officers, including the later Field Marshall Haig, set out to remedy some of the failings highlighted in South Africa. The Militia and Yeomanry were amalgamated to form the Territorial Force and, by the Haldane Act of 1907, this body came into existence and was linked directly by locality and name to the appropriate regular county-based battalions. However, they were regarded by themselves and by the army hierarchy as a separate entity, having different roles, their own officers and organization.

Coltman volunteered for the 6th battalion of the North Staffordshire Regiment, a territorial formation whose volunteers were mainly drawn from the areas between Stafford, Burton and the south Derbyshire countryside. This unit belonged to what was then known as the 1st North Midland Territorial Division, later numbered as the 46th(TF) Division: serving alongside the 5th North Staffords, mainly from the Potteries area, South Staffords from around the Black Country and Lincolns, Leicesters and Sherwood Foresters. When first formed, it had been envisaged that the Territorial Force would be used exclusively for homeland defence. Indeed, it was necessary for soldiers to volunteer to fight abroad. The demands of the Western front meant that individual battalions had gone overseas during the early battles but, at the time of Coltman's enlistment, no whole territorial division had left these shores. Unknown to these men from the Midlands their division was to be the first, landing at Le Havre in the bitterly cold final days of February 1915.

For Bill Coltman the decision to enlist must have been very difficult. Newly-married and with a baby son, he had immediate dependents for whom he was the only provider. As a devout Christian, belonging to a very disciplined Bible-orientated group he would have been fully conversant of the teachings of the Ten Commandments: 'Thou shalt not kill'.[2] However, he would have also had sufficient scriptural knowledge to have known that God had guided and blessed the armies of Israel in their wars against the heathens. That this period was the time following the blatant press propaganda which enlarged and dramatized the German army atrocities in Belgium and Northern France may or may not be a significant factor. Stories of babies being hoisted on the end of German bayonets and the wholesale shooting of civilians had been a regular feature in the newspapers and, in a time when so much was passed on by word of mouth, many of these accounts would have been added to in the telling. This was the time of going to war to protect 'little' Belgium from the 'heathen hordes'; the reality being that by now only a tiny area around Ypres (Ieper) was still in allied hands. Certainly others from the 'Brethren' rallied to the colours. From my own local Meeting at Butt Lane, Staffordshire the uncle of one of the current congregation volunteered for the 5th Battalion at the tender age of

---

2 Exodus chapter 20 verse 13. Quoted from the King James Version of the Bible.

The decision to enlist would have been one for Bill's conscience alone. Perhaps uniquely, the autonomous nature of the 'Brethren' Meetings and their lack of a central governing body would mean that each man would 'search his heart and the scriptures of truth' to decide what was the will of God for him. My own late father-in-law went through such a process in World War Two and, joining the Royal Engineers, saw action in Northern Europe from 1944 to 1945. However, the views of individual gatherings could vary. A current friend who belonged to a 'Brethren' Meeting in Wolverhampton chose to serve during post-war National Service, fighting with the UN infantry forces in Korea, while his older brother claimed exemption on religious grounds and never served. Much to my friend's surprise, his brother was respected more for his refusal than he was for his service! None of the Christians who met in that Granary in Winshill are alive today and none has left any record; we will never know what their collective attitude to the Great War was.

In January 1915 Bill Coltman was commencing his basic training in the Reserve Battalion of the 6th North Staffords. For army nomenclature purposes this was referred to as the 2/6th Battalion, its function was to serve as a holding and training battalion based in Burton, supplying trained men to the 1/6th. Training consisted of typical army drill, designed to instil unthinking obedience to commands, developing proficiency with the rifle, and especially the bayonet. Although not as long as its French counterpart, the bayonet attached to the Short Lee-Enfield Rifle was a lengthy and fierce weapon. The 'spirit of the bayonet' was emphasized. Regular training in charging across and plunging this frightening implement into a suspended sack of straw was seen to be vital in developing an offensive spirit. It ignored the reality that before anyone could get close enough to use it the likelihood was that he would have been

---

[3] Just 18 years old, he was to die on October 13th, 1915, and is buried in Le Cabaret Rouge Cemetery, Northern France – his grave bears the inscription 'With Christ'.

blown up by a shell or hit by machine gun fire. Almost 60% of Great War casualties were from artillery fire, less than 1% from bayonet wounds. At least for a man living in the country the living conditions during training in the winter and spring of 1915 would have been more tolerable. His work on the land from an early age would have given Bill a degree of upper body strength that would, together with the better food of the country life, have made him fitter and stronger than the average recruit of that time. Nutrition in the towns was so poor among the working classes that recruits often added over seven kilograms to their weight and two centimetres in height during their six months of basic army training. Standing at five feet, four inches, with blue eyes and fair hair Bill Coltman would be viewed as short by today's standards. Among his contemporaries he would not have stood out remarkably.

At this point we can be clear that, like all recruits to the 2/6th, Bill Coltman would have carried a rifle and learned how and when to use it effectively. Indeed, a copy of a 1915 photograph taken on Burton Railway Station shows him, together with an officer and other ranks, carrying a Lee Enfield. What we cannot ascertain with certainty is when he took the decision that was to change his life in the army. At some point between the end of his training in England and the attack on Gommecourt in July 1916 by the 46th Division, Bill decided that it would be fundamentally wrong for him to kill another human being. Sifting through the brief accounts that exist, one suggests that it was after that abortive attack that he took this decision; others suggest it was at the end of training before going abroad. My own research favours the latter view for reasons made clearer later. The reason for his request to be transferred to the Regimental Stretcher Bearers was clarified personally in a rare interview given by Bill just two years before his death. 'I don't ever regret joining up, even though, as a member of the "Christian Brethren", I absolutely refused to kill anyone'. The decision had been made; he would never change it or regret it.

Bill Coltman left the shores of Britain for the first time in his life when he was transferred with a draft from the Burton depot, to reinforce the 1/6th Battalion, part of the 46th (North Midland Division) under the command of Major-General Hon. E. J. Montague-Stuart-Wortley. Born of landed gentry in the Midlands area, Stuart-Wortley was an old-style commander with a caring attitude to men judged by Great War standards. Coltman joined the battalion following training in the Rouen area, where he had landed in June 1915. His delay in getting to the front line was fortuitous. After 'holding the line' at Messines, south of Ypres, the 46th had been moved south in September and appeared as a reserve formation in the latter stages of the Battle of Loos which had commenced on 25th September. Generally forgotten among the list of great First World War battles, Loos had been the first occasion when the volunteer and territorial divisions of the army had taken part in a large-scale attack. It had been a disaster; by the time the Midlanders arrived, thousands of men had perished in an abortive advance against a well-entrenched enemy. The Germans had learned quickly from their experience in the battle at Neuve Chapelle earlier in the year when British troops had advanced, albeit with increasing casualties. Despite the eleven thousand German defenders being outnumbered by seven to one and the first proper use of chlorine gas by the BEF, the enemy had repulsed nearly all attacks and taken a toll of over 50,000 casualties on the advancing divisions. It was a battle unwanted by Sir John French, Sir Douglas Haig, or any of the Divisional commanders, involving an attack supported by too little artillery, over ground lacking any natural cover.

Visiting Loos today, it is impossible to see how any advancing troops could have survived in the open terrain of the battlefield. Here Rudyard Kipling's son Jack was to die, causing his distraught father to visit there many times both during and after the war to seek the answer to his disappearance. Today, controversially, his body lies in a small cemetery in the middle of the open fields, some still disputing whether or not his remains really lie there.

The last throes of this terrible battle was to witness appalling losses by the 46th Division as they were sent forward on October 13th to capture the German stronghold of the Hohenzollern Redoubt.

Casualty returns for the 1/5th Battalion North Staffs alone show 105 dead. The four battalions of the Division which had taken part in the initial attack that day were effectively written off, almost half being casualties. The Guards were moved up to replace them. Many of the Potteries' lads who had charged forward that morning to the cry of 'Up the Potters!' now lay dead or wounded. Among them was Harold Breese, the young member of the 'Brethren' from Butt Lane. Many others lie in Dud Corner Cemetery or are commemorated on its walls, their remains never having been found. Surprisingly this area of the battlefield remained quiet for the next three years – perhaps both sides now realized what Stuart-Wortley had; it was unsuitable ground over which to launch an attack. However, for the dead lying out in 'No Man's Land' this resulted in most bodies never being recovered or identified.

The impact of this pointless and disastrous attack on a heavily fortified enemy strongpoint can be gauged by the casualty figures. On that terrible day, the Division, together with the attached Pioneer Battalion of the 1/1st Monmouths lost a total of 180 officers and 3583 other ranks killed, wounded or missing; 65% per cent of the men involved, including two battalion commanders, Colonel John Knight of the North Staffords and Colonel George Fowler of the Sherwood Foresters. This compared with less than two thousand losses in total during service from February to September near Ypres and at Vimy Ridge.

The 1/6th Battalion had been spared the worst of the losses on October 13th; now they returned to holding the line. Coltman, service number 241028, joined A Company around the 16th October when they were at Allouagne. This was a relatively quiet period after Loos but the battalion had to replace over 300 losses in officers and men. A week later they moved to billets at Fouquereuil and then on to Epinette. It was not until November 7th that Coltman's company moved into the front lines near to the old battlefield of Neuve Chapelle. There they took over the Brigade dugouts at 'Ludhiana Lodge', named by earlier occupants from the Indian Sirhind Brigade. This would have been Bill's first taste of trench life. The area resembled the counties from which most of the battalion came, open countryside dotted with small villages and small mining communities. Today, the Indian Memorial stands nearby with a Portuguese cemetery alongside – reminders that this war would involve a large part of the world.

Coltman's survival would have required a fast acclimatization to the ways of trench life. The trenches here were not, strictly speaking, trenches at all. The area was waterlogged for most of the year and the heavily sandbagged front line was in poor repair and fronted by a ditch, usually full of a mixture of water, barbed wire and detritus. The first few days would be the most dangerous. As a newcomer he would have needed to learn about snipers, the ever-present threat from artillery and, especially, the 'moaning minnies', the German trench mortars or *minenwerfer* which could launch a huge bomb into a trench with little accuracy but frightening consequences should it land near. Trench life was a 'quick learning curve' and Bill must have learned rapidly. As one of usually four stretcher-bearers attached to 'A' Company, he would have had to familiarize himself with the network of front-line and reserve/communication trenches. Most movement would be at night and, without a good knowledge of the immediate topography, it would be easy to become disorientated. Having been brought up and worked in the countryside he would have a 'good eye for the land', as well as a working knowledge of the position of the sun, moon and stars to help to find his way.

Stretcher-bearers were the first point of contact for a wounded or injured soldier. Despite much criticism of aspects of the army in the Great War, little has been directed at the medical services. Statistics show that the likelihood of survival for a wounded soldier was highest in the British forces, better than the enemy and far better than our French allies. There was a clearly laid down system for the evacuation and treatment of the wounded 'Tommy'. This would prove to be a significant factor in boosting morale, as well as ensuring that a large proportion of those treated could return to the front. Modern medical knowledge supports the belief that the first minutes after the soldier is wounded are the most critical with regard to survival or recovery; this is sometimes referred to as the 'golden hour'. Anyone who has experienced a sudden injury will have been aware of the physical and mental trauma involved in the first moments. Hasty attention and treatment is vital. For the wounded their first assistance would come from the company stretcher-bearers, generally 'mates' who knew them and would be able to calm nerves and apply vitally needed dressings. Getting to a casualty quickly, assessing his condition, dressing wounds and moving him rapidly for treatment was the task of the soldier with 'SB' on his arm. How well he did this could mean life or death – too slowly and the victim died; too thoughtlessly and the 'angel of mercy' himself might be the one to perish.

The period from November 30th to December 4th was spent in the front line. This may not seem to be a very long time but five days within a hundred metres of the enemy, observed during the day and busy during the night would be very wearing on the mind and body. Just the need for constant vigilance, combined with the lack of sleep, could make men careless and that could and did lead to casualties. In addition, the withdrawing enemy had opportunity to choose the better ground in which to construct their trench lines which were usually deeper, better drained and containing superior dugouts and shelters. This was the period of the war when the enemy artillery, trench mortars and machine guns were far more plentiful and of a superior quality. Although a relatively quiet sector of the front, it was the policy of the British to seek to dominate 'no man's land'; the area between the two front lines. Using the protection of moonless nights, raiding parties, led by a subaltern or senior non-commissioned officer, would go out and seek to capture enemy troops or cause damage to trenches. Wiring parties and the digging of sap trenches out towards the enemy would be other nocturnal activities. Wounded men unable to move, would often lie in between the lines and the company stretcher bearers would be expected to retrieve them, often under enemy fire and shelling.

Most of December was spent in the usual routine of marching and training away from the front line, living in a variety of billets. On

Christmas Day, units of the 46th Division, including the Staffordshire Brigade, found themselves on the move. Spending nights at Abbeville, Villeneave and Montereau, they reached the embarkation port of Marseilles on the 28th; having a spell at   Santi Camp before embarkation on the SS Beltana on the 5th of January 1916 – destination Egypt. Malta was reached on the 8th, before landing at Alexandria on 12th January. One thing was certain for Bill and his comrades; it was a lot hotter and safer than France in January!

Chapter Four

'Out of Egypt I have called my Son',
Matthew chapter 2 verse 15

The year 1916 opened with Bill Coltman and his unit arriving in Alexandria and moving to Shalluta station, the nearby camp, and then by train to Sidi Bardia on the 30th. Events had overtaken the reasons for their transfer to North Africa; the Dardenelles campaign had ended only weeks before so they were no longer required for the protection of the Suez Canal from Turkish forces. This task was given to the 42nd Division, recently evacuated from the peninsula. By February 5th they were embarking on the HMT Transylvania, sailing back through the Mediterranean to arrive in Marseilles six days later. For the troops it had been a pleasant winter holiday compared with the Western Front, although the winter cruises had not been without undersea hazards!

Holiday over, it was soon back to work. By February 13th the 1/6th were at Pont Lemy in France and, after billets at Longvillers, the battalion marched to Longuevillette. The BEF, newly commanded by General, later Field Marshall Sir Douglas Haig, had agreed to take over a longer portion of the line, freeing French forces for the planned major spring offensive. On March 12th the division took over trenches at Neuville St Vaast, a six day stay flanked by the 51st Division on the right and the 138th to the left. After billets nearby, it was back to the front line from 24th to 30th March before marching north to join the Divisional Reserve at Ecoivres. This gives us a clear picture of how life was for the 'Tommy' in the middle period of the Great War on the western front; a rotation from reserve to support and then the front line. From his arrival in June 1915 Private Coltman had spent just 25 days in the front line out of nine months. He had yet to be involved in a major battle. However, this was to change in just a few weeks. He would be take his place in the battle synonymous with the Great War in France.

On the 29th April, the 46th Division staff had its first intimation that the unit was on the move. They were to journey south into the far point of the Third Army's area, near a village called Gommecourt. The British Third Army was commanded by General Edmund Allenby, a distant descendant of Oliver Cromwell and a former Cavalry Corps Commander. He had a reputation for being harsh on discipline and insensitive to heavy casualties. In moving to this area, the division would come under the corps command of Lieutenant-General T.D. Snow, grandfather of television presenters Jon and Peter. This would involve adapting to new surroundings and a new command structure. Most of the 'Tommies' were unconcerned about this; glad to know they were leaving this unpleasant area. As part of 137th Brigade, the North Staffordshires were the first to move and, upon arrival in pleasant early spring weather, found their new venue to be a vast improvement on what they had left behind. This was a notoriously quiet part of the front, occupied by the French until quite recently and obviously subject to a 'live and let live' policy. The Divisional rest and training area around Lucheux was particularly pleasant with streams and woodland; a lovely place to be in spring.

Two factors, however, spoiled this haven of rest: the need to improve and dig new trench lines, and the onset of a particularly high level of sickness among the troops. Many men began to complain of high temperatures, vomiting and diarrhoea. At first this was thought to have been paratyphoid or enteric fever; later it was diagnosed as a form of 'trench fever' passed on by lice, always present in the warm, moist and soiled clothing the soldiers wore. Fever, headache and dizziness would affect men to varying degrees for up to a week; then improvement would be followed by its return. This could incapacitate for as long as two months before clearing the body. Indeed, without rest, good sanitation and healthy diet, men could be permanently rendered unfit and over 10% were sent home for good. For some, the illness was fatal. To counter this a regime of vapour and steam cleansing baths was instituted by Lieutenant-Colonel Beevor M.O. and the result was a gradual reduction in cases. With hindsight, it is likely that the poor sanitation and cleanliness of the billets near Neuville St Vaast was the source of the infection. The result was that many men were weakened and the burden of work for the fit was increased.

On June 30th 1916, just over twelve months after leaving Burton, Bill's unit found itself moving from billets in Humbercamp to relieve the 4th Leicestershire Battalion. They marched to a village named Fonquevillers, known to the men as 'Funky villas'. They had been there before. During the early summer months of May and June, it was a pleasant enough place, although unseasonably wet it was a quiet part of the line, the ploughed fields resembling south-eastern England.

Nearby there was a meandering river – it was called the River Somme!

Millions of words have been written about the July 1st attack by the BEF on the Somme. It was the worst day for casualties in the history of the British army. Faulty intelligence, unreliable ammunition, uncut wire and steadfast German defence meant that nearly 60,000 casualties were suffered, nearly a third dead. Most were lost in the first two hours of the attack. Closer examination shows that the results of the advance were not uniform all along the nearly twenty miles of front involved. To the south, adjacent to the French army, some clear progress was made. Further north, this was not the case. The 46th were part of General 'Bull' Allenby's 3rd Army at the very northern extreme of the chosen front. Attacking with the 56th Division, they were to take part in an envelopment of the fortified German-held village of Gommecourt. This was meant to be diversionary, intended to draw enemy forces away from the main attack to the south. To achieve this, the troops occupying the line prior to the attack had been instructed to make their preparations obvious to the enemy! Now the 46th Division was expected to destroy a fortified strongpoint without any element of surprise; difficult if the wire had been cut[4] and the defenders destroyed by

---

[4] The matter of wire cutting was a very important issue; the 1914-18 war

the week-long bombardment; impossible when these aims had not been achieved.

The 56th achieved a remarkable advance, managing to invest part of the village but the 46th achieved little. Taking heavy casualties, their commander, who had witnessed the horrors of the Loos attack, refused to commit his full force, undoubtedly saving many lives. However, it was to cost him his command; Major-General Montague-Stuart-Wortley bore the blame and returned to England. Despite Haig's appraisal that the Division had not attacked forcefully enough 1/6th Battalion North Staffs' casualties had been significant: of less than a thousand men involved over 250 had been killed or wounded, terrible by modern standards but small compared to the suffering of some battalions on the 1st July 1916. Bill Coltman's contribution was significant. Throughout the day, he had been busy carrying out his first aid and recovery work. This was his first experience of a major battle and it was the biggest attack that the BEF had ever mounted. As evening approached it was clear even to the rank and file that the attack on Gommecourt village had not succeeded; enemy troops and artillery were still 'plastering' them, and most of the wounded were still out in 'No Man's Land' under fire and suffering badly from pain and thirst. Although tired and, having been under intense fire for nearly twelve hours, Bill was still out near the German front line taking shelter in a shell hole together with a group of other men. Like many others, the most sensible course of action would have been to stay there until dusk but there was a problem; one of the group had been wounded and it was unlikely he would survive that long.

---

was the first where armies had made widespread use of barbed wire, the German version being particularly unpleasant. By this period of the war barbed wire would run in thick bands in front of both sets of trenches. At Gommecourt the British wire alone was in a band of about 40 metres depth. When 'going over the top' wire proved to be a major obstacle; paths had to be opened in the British wire and enemy wire destroyed. The BEF's shrapnel shells proved incapable of this in 1916.

Deciding that it was vital to return this badly wounded sergeant to his own lines, Coltman lifted the man on his back and crawled approximately seventy metres back to the British frontline. However, having got this man back to safety, Bill went out again and rescued another casualty, safely returning in a similar fashion. Now, exhausted but relatively safe in his own trenches, he could have legitimately felt that 'he had done his bit' and kept his head down. Within minutes he heard another cry for help and, again, left his position to drag another back; sadly, this effort was futile for the victim joined the ranks of those never to return from France. In his first experience of a major battle, Private William Coltman had already shown devotion to duty. On a day when many acts of bravery would be carried out, this may have been seen as only doing his job, but it would be the prelude to another brave act later that month, earning him a Mention in Dispatches, the first of his many awards for gallantry.

By now Coltman had spent over a year on active service, including the experience of one of the bloodiest battles of the war. For some, this would be regarded as meritorious service – for Bill it was only the beginning. From July 21st until 27th the battalion was in the front line trenches at Ransart. As the Somme offensive continued, the fighting became more active and ferocious in the trench lines. A new forward sap trench was being dug and was attracting enemy artillery and small arms' fire. The battalion medical officer had moved forward into a front-line dugout where a number of casualties had been taken. The stretcher-bearers were busy that day but Coltman's dedication to his duty led him to go out into 'No Man's Land' on six occasions and carry wounded men to this advance post for medical treatment. Having returned to the relative safety of the trench, he was then informed that another casualty was lying out in between the lines; without hesitation, he crawled out to the man and carried him back single-handedly, exposing himself to fire by lifting him on his back. This was to become Bill's trademark. Dispensing with the stretcher, he would place wounded men over his shoulder and carry them back, seeking 'dead' ground out of view of the enemy but often exposing himself to fire.

Not content with his efforts that day he went out in the twilight, recovering three more soldiers before scouring the area at night, even bringing back a German machine gun. For this day of conspicuous bravery in the face of the enemy, William Coltman received a Mention in Dispatches. Let those who may believe that medals were won easily in the Great War consider that fact. Ten soldiers and an enemy machine gun recovered – but Bill would have simply felt that he was doing the 'soft job' he had opted to do. His behaviour during these acts of bravery and devotion to duty would be indicative of the way in which he approached his tasks throughout the war. He was in France to serve his God; anything, therefore, that needed to be done must be carried out to the best of his ability. To quote a modern expression, 'Only the best is good enough!' It was God who must be satisfied in all things. No better way to show the reality of God's saving grace than in snatching men from a lingering death in 'No Man's Land'.

On July 27th Bill and his comrades welcomed their Territorial mates from the Potteries, as they were relieved and went into the Brigade Reserve, billeted at Berles. Nearly 150 of the battalion had been lost at Ransart in six days – many of these would have been dead if it had not been for Bill, the other bearers and medical staff. Between August and November the 1/6th were to spend a total of thirty-eight days in the front-line trenches at Ransart. Losses continued to mount; a particular period of hot weather in August corresponded with the enemy making the trenches 'very hot' for them. This period was punctuated by billets at Berles and periods in reserve, based at Baillentmont. Finally, on November 1st the battalion moved considerably further back into reserve, billeted at Canchy. There they spent six weeks in training and learning new techniques for bombing trenches. Wastage during the times at Ransart had averaged about 50 to 100 casualties during each 'tour', suggesting that about half the men had been killed or wounded during this last spell. In one six day period, from September 9th to 15th, over 150 casualties had occurred, most from artillery fire. This was one of the features of the Great War; as most injuries were caused by the blast of high explosive or the jagged splinters of shrapnel shells, wounds were not clean, as they were generally from bullets. One of the biggest problems for the medical services in the age before penicillin was that these awful wounds were often infected by pieces of dirty clothing driven into the gash or cut. This led to what is known as 'gas gangrene', serious infection often requiring amputation if wounds were not cleaned quickly and effectively. It made speedy evacuation even more important. Most front line troops knew and respected the men who carried no weapons but shared the privations and dangers to save their mates.

This is a good point to stop and consider the conditions which men like Bill Coltman endured in the trenches of the Western front. Although living below ground had its privations and difficulties, it was the only way to survive in view of the weapons of mass killing which had been developed before and during the war. Artillery fire, snipers, trench mortars, grenades and gas were now in widespread use by both sides. Additionally, this was the period of mining, particularly in the areas where Bill's battalion served. The enemy had first tunnelled under the ground and blown up trenches in the La Bassee area during 1915. The BEF had responded fitfully at first, the Royal Engineers not being experienced in this line of work owing to the mobile nature of the pre-war army. An enterprising business man named Norton Griffiths had offered his services to the BEF. Driving around northern France in his pink Rolls-Royce, he spoke to senior officers and arranged to bring over a large number of miners from Britain, many of whom had worked on the London Underground system. Paid over seven times the daily rate of a 'Tommy', these men quickly redressed the balance and 1916 into 1917 became the 'heyday' for mining activities. This would culminate in the July 1st Somme explosions at scenes such as Hawthorn Ridge and later at Messines in June 1917 when the explosion of nineteen huge mines would obliterate the ridge, the sound being heard in southern England. This potentially fatal occurrence at any time of day or night was an added psychological burden, together with the damp and wet, lack of fresh food and infestation by lice and rats. Truly, no soldiers of any era before or since have faced such widespread and constant stress. Today, we know that many could not stand it indefinitely and cracked under the pressures – generally referred to as shell-shock or battle fatigue. It is amazing to think that Bill Coltman endured such conditions for nearly four years with little relief. Just last week as I write a sudden loss of water supplies to the area where I live plunged my 22-year old son into a panic because he could not have a shower before going out, illustrating the endurance and hardiness of the 1914-18 soldier of all nations. Undoubtedly, the men of that era were not used to the degree of 'home comforts' we enjoy; they were better equipped to 'rough it'. However, perhaps there was more to Bill's ability to cope than simply that.

Coltman had volunteered to carry out a job which involved the finding and saving of those who were in great need. The nature of the Great War weaponry and the enemy's desire to wound rather than kill meant that a large proportion of men were wounded rather than killed outright. A seriously injured casualty was of more value to the enemy, since he would occupy valuable resources in his evacuation, treatment and rehabilitation, particularly if unable to return to active service. We shall never know how many casualties died of wounds because they were either never found or discovered too late. During an advance, soldiers were instructed not to stop and tend to their wounded comrades; it removed them from action and slowed the pace of the attack. The regimental stretcher bearer was to find and to recover these men as soon as possible; to do so he must always balance speed with his own exposure to danger. To be effective the bearer had to be prepared to face his own death in order to save others. This was a picture of the Christian gospel, so beloved of Bill. His commitment reflected that of his Master.

On December 10th the battalion moved to 'Funky villas' once again, bringing back far from fond memories for those who could remember the previous July. Once again their front line duty was punctuated by enemy artillery bombardments. By Christmas Day the battalion had suffered nearly a hundred casualties and they had not even been involved in a battle. 1916 ended with them billeted at St Armand. For Bill Coltman the next year would see further action and the award of his first three medals for bravery under fire.

Chapter Five

'Thy shield and exceeding great reward', Genesis chapter 15 verse 1

As the new year of 1917 arrived 1/6th Battalion were at billets in Pommier before spells of front line trench duty during January. On February 3rd began a new 'tour' which saw them alternating with the 1/5th North Staffs and 2/7th London Battalions in trenches at Monchy le Preux. Here was a small salient or bulge in the line which invited German attempts to remove it. Life was a lot more exciting than it had been earlier in the winter and casualties both in the front line and support trenches were correspondingly greater. On the 17th the newly-promoted Lance-Corporal Coltman was to carry out the acts of bravery which led to his first medal award.

The weather had been cold, dry and misty and this encouraged Captain Norman Hipkins to lead a small party of men into 'No Man's Land' to repair the British barbed wire emplacements about sixty metres in front of the trench line. Suddenly the mist began to clear and the party gradually became visible to the Germans, less than 200 metres away. Rifle and machine gun fire opened up and the officer in charge ordered the troops to retire immediately to the safety of their own line. In the tradition of 'leading from the front', Captain Hipkins was the last to retire and, as he was passing through the wire, he was hit in the thigh by rifle fire and fell, unable to move. Exposed as he was, it was only a matter of time before he would be hit again and probably killed. Bill Coltman, witnessing this, left the trench immediately, crawled under fire to the stricken officer, extricated him from the barbed wire entanglement and dragged him safely back. During this rescue he placed his own body between that of Captain Hipkins and the enemy. For this act of bravery he was awarded the Military Medal, the citation being published in the London Gazette a week later. The MM, together with the Military Cross (the officers' equivalent award) had been introduced early in the Great War. It was regarded by the troops as a lesser award than either the coveted Distinguished Conduct Medal or the rare Victoria Cross, both of which, unlike the MM and MC were linked to a lifetime pension.

When, 44 years after the war, Bill was honoured by Burton Council the ceremony was attended by Mr Herbert Hipkins, the older brother of the now deceased officer whose life Bill had saved.

A single conspicuous act of bravery had led to the award of his first medal; his second would recognize a series of actions over a period of several days when the Company stretcher bearer would defy death many times. March and April saw 46th Division moving around in holding the line between Monchy and their old battleground of Gommecourt. On the 1st of May the Battalion moved to front line trenches at Lens, within sight of their first 'baptism of fire' at Loos nearly two years before. At 4am on a quiet Spring morning, they occupied the front line with their own 1/5th Battalion on their left and the 10th Canadian Brigade to the right. Within hours, the enemy greeted the newcomers with salvoes of heavy shelling, causing casualties of ten dead and two wounded, a ratio illustrating the deadly effects of heavy artillery fire.

A week later the battalion was to be involved in one of their fiercest engagements of the war, so much so that they regard it as a battle honour alongside Loos, Gommecourt and the battles of the 'last hundred days'. The 1/6th had moved into the front trenches on the line of the Lens-Lieven Road. On May 8th, their first day there, they decided to give a 'welcome' to the enemy opposite. Trenches here afforded better protection, as there were a series of underground shelters just behind in which troops could shelter. These may have been the remains of old tunnel workings, for the area was the scene of concentrated mining by both sides during the previous two years. 'A' company occupied these places of refuge and three and four platoons were ordered to move along towards the forward sap trenches and announce their arrival by bombing the Germans in the opposing front lines. This required surprise and stealth but, just as the men were moving into position, the Canadian battalion on the immediate right chose to open fire. The enemy, now alert, responded vigorously; signal flares lit up the sky, artillery and machine gun fire rained down on the front lines. Almost immediately, a large mortar shell landed in the entrance of one of the old tunnels, killing outright two sentries. The two platoon officers were dazed. Sheltering inside with them was Coltman, knocked to the ground by the blast which removed his steel helmet. Otherwise unharmed, he attended to the officers and, having checked them over, began to move about, tending to and removing the wounded.

Finally, he moved to the tunnel entrance to examine one of the sentries and, as he reached the bottom of the steps, a further mortar bomb exploded nearby, causing the roof of the tunnel to collapse. Shaken but again unwounded, Bill got to his feet to see how else he could help; already his prompt action had prevented further casualties but now more was to follow. One of the officers called for a volunteer to go back to Company Headquarters to appraise and report on the situation. To leave the shelter of the trenches at night was dangerous enough but now the early May dawn was approaching; to be out in the light was tantamount to suicide. Unhesitatingly, Bill offered to go. He said afterwards that he chose to crawl over the ground rather than work his way back because it was quicker and probably safer! Having arrived at Company HQ this brave man led the Medical Officer, Captain Hannah back to the scene, where he was able to tend the ten wounded; sadly the two sentries and two other men were beyond earthly help.

Later in the month, on May 24th 'B' and 'D' Companies were called upon to make a large trench raid near to a place known as Nash Valley. 'A' and 'C' Companies were in reserve but, as a very experienced man, Bill Coltman was asked to reconnoitre the ground in order to find a suitable place for Captain Hannah to set up an advanced dressing station so that wounded could be seen quickly.[5]

---

[5] Those who wish to know more should consult ALAN MACDONALD's masterly and comprehensive account of the 46th Division *A Lack of Offensive Spirit?*, Iona Books, 2008. This deals with the medical

The raid was successful but casualties occurred; Coltman had managed to locate an old dug out between the two front lines and here the M.O. operated. The stretcher bearers moved forward and back between the lines helping wounded and taking them to the ADS. Just after a retaliatory barrage had lifted, one terribly wounded man was found, shrapnel had torn a gaping gash in his forearm, breaking it in several places and severing an artery. Bill and his team applied emergency treatment, staunched the blood flow and carried him back. Bill recalled, many years later, that very soon after the soldier was sitting up, calmly smoking a cigarette. This probably meant that his front line service was over – his wound was a 'ticket to Blighty' – so easily it could have meant an early grave. At this point we might mention that Bill Coltman's religious beliefs would have caused him to be a teetotaller and a non-smoker, rare today but not that uncommon in 1917, except in the front line.

The ongoing feature of life in the line near Lens was the heavy shelling experienced. On June 6th 'A' Company was given the task of rewiring in front of a particular 'hotspot' called 'Bugs Alley'. This drew a fierce response from the enemy who began to shell the area heavily. An exploding trench mortar bomb set fire to a dump of stored Very lights. The following series of explosions caused many casualties and Coltman and other stretcher bearers disregarded their own safety to reach, tend and remove the wounded. On the next morning, a German trench mortar landed a bomb directly on the nearby 'D' company HQ. Casualties occurred immediately and all the officers were hit; the company commander, Captain Hogarth, was killed and 2/Lieutenant Wilkinson died from wounds. The dugout caved in, resting men were buried, including a number of the stretcher bearers. 'A' Company were in reserve and Coltman led the stretcher bearers in a successful attempt to reach the men in the collapsed bunker and release the wounded and dead within.

---

arrangements prior to the July 1st attack at Gommecourt, illustrating how the effectiveness of casualty evacuation and treatment was often due to the local initiative of Divisional and Battalion M.O.s.

One week later, enemy shelling led to a tunnel in a railway embankment where men were sheltering being hit and collapsing, burying the occupants. Coltman led a party to the tunnel entrance. What they saw was an awful scene; men had been blown apart by the blast, others had been suffocated by the collapse or lost limbs to the falling debris. The men continued to work, Coltman not resting until all twelve occupants had been removed. Sadly, nine were dead but the lives of the others were undoubtedly saved by prompt and brave action. For this series of actions Lance-Corporal William Coltman was awarded a bar to his Military Medal. The citation began:

'In the trenches near Lens; this NCO (Stretcher-Bearer) has shown great gallantry, devotion to duty and disregard for personal danger on three following occasions'.

It then goes on to list Coltman's exploits on June 6th, June 7th and June 14th as outlined above. Note the three elements of the citation illustrating his bravery, duty and disregard for himself – a fitting tribute indeed!

At this point let us digress from the main narrative to look at the general situation on the Western front in the latter half of 1917. The previous year had witnessed the rapid expansion of the BEF in Belgium and France. They now had responsibility for holding just under 40% of the trench line, less than the French, but it must be remembered that the British portion included some of the most active parts of the front. The so-called Ypres salient, a bulge in the line around the one remaining Belgian town not in enemy hands, was a constant drain on British resources, as they had the main responsibility for holding it. It is too easy to view the British High Command as a group of upper class gentry sitting far behind the lines in comfort and consigning men to death in hastily-planned and fruitless attacks on impregnable German lines.

The strategic initiative had been grasped by the enemy in 1914 when their six week advance had taken them almost to the River

Seine. The 'miracle of the Marne' had removed the danger to Paris but still left the invaders in control of nearly all Belgium and a significant area of Northern France. Not only did this give the Germans access to industry and raw material, it also allowed them to use many of the male population as workers in the construction of trenches and defensive strongpoints. The retreating army in 1914 had been able to select excellent positions for the sites of their defensive emplacements and supporting artillery. The widespread and mass production of barbed wire, guns and ammunition had enabled all combatants to be able to protect   their lines easily. Tinned food had allowed warfare to continue through the winter months, albeit generally on a lesser scale. The imperative had been from the first year of the war for the allied armies to advance and throw the enemy off the territory they had taken by force. This was the moral and strategic aim which informed allied thinking.

During April, 1917, the BEF had taken the offensive around Arras in support of a new French attack launched in the Chemin de Dames region. This had been planned and was to be implemented by a new and exciting French Commander Robert Nivelle who had won fame in the defence of the fortress of Verdun in 1916. To clarify the strategic position, the placement of the armies demanded that the allies attack, often over terrain well suited to the enemy defenders. In addition, the large British efforts at Loos, the Somme and Arras in early 1917 had all been at the behest of France and designed to support French plans and initiatives. Now, the Germans, with knowledge of the impending French offensive, withdrew along a large part of the front to new positions, built in the main by labour from the occupied zone. This new line became known to the BEF as the Hindenburg Line, named after the recently-appointed Commander-in-Chief of the German army there. The 'scorched earth' policy applied to the evacuated areas was to deny any resources to the allies and to hinder any advance. The subsequent French attack was a disaster; Nivelle was effectively dismissed and replaced by Petain whose first task was to restore morale among many French units who now refused to leave the safety of their trenches. The effect of this was to place a greater demand on the resources of the

BEF, both in holding the line and taking the attack to the enemy. By now the promising battle at Arras had become a wearing-out affair, replacing advance with attrition. The third full summer of the war approached with the German army still holding the strategic initiative. With the French army in disarray, the burden fell on the BEF to launch the main offensives, or to hold on until the American forces arrived in France.

For the 46th Division their 'failure' at Gommecourt in 1916 was to have repercussions. Sir Douglas Haig, the Commander-in-Chief of the BEF regarded them as an unreliable unit, a view he had of territorial battalions generally unless they had proved otherwise. Even in the now greatly expanded army, unit distinctions still existed. The Guards, 51st Highland Regiment, together with the old regular army battalions were regarded as the best. This was a dubious honour, as they, together with the Canadians and the ANZACS were often in the forefront of attacks, taking the highest casualties. This would mean that the 46th would not be involved in any of the four main British offensives of 1917; Arras in April; Messines in June; Ypres in July or Cambrai in November. Most of the Staffordshire men were probably not sorry to have missed them; they took little ground and ran up a casualty list of over a million killed, wounded and missing. This did not, however, mean that life was pleasant in the line; by June 27th Bill Coltman and the 1/6th were back in their familiar surroundings of the Lens-Lieven Road. During the subsequent three days, they were involved in heavy fighting, including counterattacks by German troops. Casualties began to mount steadily and Bill was heavily involved in the finding and recovery of wounded from between the lines. During this time, nearly 120 of the battalion were killed or wounded; when they were relieved by their Potteries' mates from the 1/5th on the night of the 29th, Coltman refused to retire with his unit but stayed on the battlefield, scouring it for wounded under the cover of darkness. Exhausted, by the morning he had satisfied himself that all living casualties had been recovered. When he returned, he had over thirty pay books belonging to the battalion dead, a testimony to his determination to save as many as possible. For his gallant service during this time, William Coltman was

awarded the Distinguished Conduct Medal (DCM). The citation read: 'For the most conspicuous gallantry and devotion to duty. During operations south-west of Lens between 28th of June and 2nd July, 1917, Lance-Corporal Coltman's conduct was magnificent. He assisted in evacuating several badly wounded men from the front line, and worked untiringly until every wounded man had been taken out. He undoubtedly, by his action, saved the lives of several of these men, as otherwise they would have had to lie up in the front line without proper attention. During the night, he searched the ground between and in front of trenches we had captured, and under shell and machine gun fire, he brought in any men who had been wounded. Lance-Corporal Coltman's absolute indifference to danger and gallant conduct had a very inspiring effect on the rest of the men and was a splendid example to them. I cannot speak too highly of this NCO's gallantry on this and previous occasions'.
No. 241028 L/Cpl. W.H.Coltman, DCM, MM and Bar, 1/6th Battalion North Staffordshire Regiment.

Just after Coltman's DCM was gazetted on 23rd July, he was to suffer his only injury of the war. On July 2nd the battalion left the area around the Lens- Lieven Road and went back to Bully Grenay for rest, training, and arrival of replacements. A week later they marched to billets in the village of Brauy and while there, on 11th July they were inspected by His Majesty King George V. It is unknown whether the recent DCM winner was introduced to the King; less than two years later the two would meet again at Buckingham Palace – there an introduction definitely occurred. Following this inspection 1/6th Battalion rested in billets at Raimbert before moving forward once more to take over trenches near Hulluch. A spell of five relatively quiet days there was followed by moving back to new billets in reserve at Noyelles. By now the routine of trench life would have been familiar: five or six days in the front line followed by a similar period in reserve and rest, recuperation every three to four weeks behind the lines. However, even rest in billets could be hazardous, as the heavier German artillery guns could launch shells over ten miles. Therefore, even nearby villages could be unsafe.

On August 4th Bill's unit entered billets in Noyelles for a short rest. While there, the village was subjected to long-range artillery fire. The Battalion stretcher bearers were enjoying (or enduring) a lecture in a village house when an eight inch German shell exploded just outside; a second struck a house nearby where there were civilians. This building collapsed, burying a young girl, a five year old boy and their mother. Despite the risk of further shelling and a further collapse of the building, Bill Coltman and the other bearers dashed in and recovered the mother and her daughter, shaken and badly bruised but alive. The little boy could not be seen among the debris. Coltman stayed in the house alone, searching the rubble until he discovered the lad underneath the collapsed chimney breast, uninjured but distressed. The troops were able to give assistance to the villagers. Although six civilians died many others were saved by their prompt action.

Around this period, it is not known exactly when it occurred, Coltman was to be affected by gas poisoning when, during a 'quiet' time in the trenches, a special Royal Engineers Company appeared under orders to strafe the enemy trenches with gas projectiles. The appearance of these units was dreaded by the men. While their success was variable, what was certain was that the enemy would retaliate forcefully. Just after they commenced operations a mis-fire occurred and a soldier was hurt by the firing ring from one of the shells. Coltman treated the man and sent him back to the dressing station. Now, the retaliation began; artillery shells landed in the trench and set fire to the gas shell dump causing a cloud of toxic fumes to spread. Some ten men nearby were affected before they could apply their protective headgear. Coltman went to their assistance, having donned his gas mask. However, the cloud lingered for a long period and exposure led to Bill being affected by the fumes. For the only time in the war he was led away for treatment. He was absent from the line for two weeks before being passed fit for duty.

In considering the life of William Coltman VC, one of the most amazing factors was his sheer capacity to endure the long-term hardships of trench life. When we look at the Great War career of most 'old soldiers' who have left us a record, we notice that for many of them their front-line Western front experience added up to just a few weeks or months at most. There are exceptions, Frank Richards and Edmund Blunden among them, but Coltman served for a period of just over three years in France, spending at least a quarter of that time in trench lines. When life expectancy could be as little a two weeks during the campaigns of 1916 to 1918, this is a remarkable achievement. His fortnight out of action due to gas must have been a blessed relief and an opportunity to relax away from the danger and the carnage of the front.

Some may point out that he was, perhaps, fortunate not to experience a major battle; not 'going over the top' between Gommecourt in 1916 and the Hindenburg Line in the 'last hundred days' but as a regimental stretcher bearer he was exposed to danger whenever casualties demanded attention and, as we have seen, this was a frequent occurrence in the day-to-day experience in the line. To have endured that constant exposure to danger, particularly the terrifying nature of artillery and mortar fire, must have demanded a great deal of resilience. We have no record of his times on leave in Britain. We can assume that these would have occurred about every nine months and lasted for three to five days – a brief, tantalising return to a 'world far different from France'. How would he have viewed those who remained at home, particularly those of his own brethren who had stayed in 'Blighty' safe from the realities of the war? One of the recurring themes in wartime soldiers' accounts is the enormity of the gap between the front line soldier and the population at home. Reading a poem such as Sassoon's 'Tanks' illustrates this. Certainly his family and friends alive today do not recall his making his views known to them. The picture we have is of a man bearing 'his lot' as Christ had borne the cross.

For Coltman and the North Staffords, 1917 came to an end in a very similar way to which it had begun. Battalion trench diaries show that the autumn and winter was spent in 'holding the line'. Hulluch, Loos and Mazingarbe appear frequently. In early September the unit was near Vermelles and took casualties in violent bombing attacks by the enemy. On September 20th they were within sight of the Double Curassier at Loos, a pit winding structure which dominated the landscape as it had done almost exactly two years earlier when fellow Staffordshire soldiers had fallen 'going over the top'. Perhaps some of their comrades took time to visit their makeshift graves. Visiting this area ninety years after the Loos offensive, it is obvious that little has changed in this quiet mining area. Between Vermelles and Hulluch stands the 46th Division memorial on the edge of the open countryside where so many lie buried – a simple cross, in need of minor repairs, a short inscription reminding us of the sacrifice of the living and the dead from the Midlands of England.

A visit today can seem so pleasant and peaceful on a September morning until, talking to those bearing flowers, you are reminded of the horror, pain, and suffering which once marred this place. For Bill Coltman, a man of the land, this would be familiar ground; by now he had spent weeks there and he would have known every fold, every shell hole that might provide a temporary cover from enemy fire. I recall a British army officer, interviewed in the aftermath of the capture of Port Stanley during the Falklands War. Under accurate Argentinian artillery fire, he told of how he hugged the ground and how his thoughts went back to the 'Tommies' of years before.

The year of 1917 had promised much but delivered little. British offensives at Arras, Ypres and Cambrai had petered out into attrition. Although the United States of America had entered the war in April, few troops had yet arrived. Ominously, the collapse of Russia had freed over a million German troops from the eastern front. These would now be available to be used in the coming year. With the French army still recovering from the failed spring offensive, the bulk of the effort would be demanded from the BEF.

Chapter Six

'The valley of the shadow of death',
Psalm 23 verse 4

The year 1918 would turn out to be a momentous one for the BEF and for Lance-Corporal William Coltman, DCM, MM and Bar. By the end of it the British army was to win more battle honours than at any time in its history, the 46th Division would gain fame and prestige by 'breaking the Hindenburg Line' and Bill would end the war as the most decorated NCO of the conflict. It is certain, however, that the greatest of optimists could not have foretold this on January 1st. Each New Year of the war had arrived with great hopes for the allied powers, only for them to be dashed in the ensuing carnage. The Cambrai offensive, which had brought the previous year to a disappointing close was typical – great initial success followed by the inevitable German recovery and counter-attack, often regaining the lost ground which had been taken at such cost.

For the 1/6th Battalion North Staffordshire Regiment, January 1st was spent in familiar surroundings. In Divisional Reserve at Noueux Les Mines, they were still near enough to be harried by long-range enemy artillery but far away enough to celebrate after a fashion. Their stay was a quiet one before a spell in the support lines at Hulluch before returning to the Reserve. This was repeated, front line service only being required for four days at Hulluch during the month. The winter weather brought greater discomfort from the cold and wet, especially the icy winds of that month, but at least it was balanced to a degree by the harder, frosty ground and the fewer vermin and absence of flies which in the hotter weather grew large and bloated on the corpses disinterred by the regular shelling.

The costly battles of 1917, when the BEF had suffered heavy casualties, led to the need to re-organize battalions to conserve manpower. This took place for the 46th Division from January 24th to February 15th when they were pulled back to Fouquieres to enable these changes to be made. This was a difficult time for morale. The British army had fostered the raising of spirits among its men by encouraging a great pride in their unit, battalion or regiment. Battalions were often the largest formation where soldiers could get to know and trust comrades and commanders. The New Armies, formed by Kitchener (now dead having drowned en route to Russia in 1916) had included large elements of so-called 'Pals' Battalions – men from the same neighbourhood who had enlisted, trained and fought together. Sadly, this had led to many 'dying together' and this had led to a rethink over the practice. Now it was policy to form units from as diverse a geographical area as possible although Welsh, Scottish and Irish   battalions retained a strong Celtic influence. The re-organization saw the disappearance and transferring of some formations and this was resented by some, especially the Territorials whose tradition had always been rooted in their local foundations. For the 46th Division, re-organization resulted in one battalion being transferred from each brigade. A new 59th North Midland Division had been formed in September 1917 in England. These were second-line units mirroring the 46th in composition. The 1/4th Lincolns, 1/7th Sherwood Foresters and their comrades from the 1/5th North Staffs joined this new division. Thus are the fortunes of war; while the 46th continued to serve in quiet areas, this new division would feel the full fury of the German offensives in March and April. Most of them would be dead, wounded or captured by May.

After re-organization, the Division enjoyed a rest in Corps Reserve, a long way back at Lisbourg. Although enjoying safety here, there would be little time to rest. They were trained in the new defensive tactics planned for the coming year. Learning from German practice, the BEF would abandon its traditional strongly-held trench line and adopt a 'defence-in-depth' approach which would see strongpoints dotted along the front, mutually supporting with machine gun fire. The front line would be thinly-held, the aim being to slow down rather than stop an enemy advance. Behind would be two further zones where the enemy was to be resisted, fought to exhaustion and then counter-attacked to regain lost ground. With hindsight, this change in tactics may look sensible – to the 'Tommy' it seemed less so. The close camaraderie and contact promoted a sense of safety. Many troops in these outposts felt vulnerable and alone. The more knowledgeable recognized that survival in the front zone was unlikely if the enemy came in force. They felt like sacrificial lambs.

On March 5th the battalion moved into the front line at Beuvry, near to the La Bassee canal. During their eight day stay they suffered casualties of three dead and one wounded before moving back into reserve at Le Preol, being relieved by the 1/5th South Staffordshires. By now the allied high command had intelligence of the timing of the expected German attack, although they could not be sure where it would fall. On Thursday, March 21st, Coltman and his battalion moved up to Cuinchy to relieve the 1/6th South Staffs. Further to the south, the most intense and concentrated artillery barrage of the war to-date could be heard from 4.40am, the immediate prelude to an attack which would drive a forty mile wedge into the BEF in the area where the Third and Fifth Armies met. While some units, particularly in the northern area, held fast and slowed the enemy advance, others, mainly those defending unfinished strongpoints in the south, fled hurriedly before the German onslaught. At this point the Battalion War Diary becomes a blank. With units moved to and fro to relieve, hold and counter-attack, it is unsurprising that no time could be found to fill in daily records!

The German offensive was finally brought to a halt. Further attacks in the north and south were held at great cost to both sides. A detailed account of these times would be superfluous here. The most direct involvement 46th Division had was when the second offensive, codenamed 'Georgette' by the German High Command, hit the area just to the north of them. This became known to the BEF as the Battle of the Lys. Detail is sketchy but it was a busy time for the Division although they were spared the terrible losses which affected some units. The third attack struck the Chemin Des Dames area where the defensive forces were mainly French. The German army had played its 'last card', although two further offensives followed in the south. Now, with the line still holding and the

American forces beginning to arrive in small but significant numbers, the initiative switched to the allies.

While the BEF waited to build up its forces and equipment for the coming offensives, 46th Division spent May, June and July in trenches just to the south of its familiar area of northern France, around Gorre, Vaudricourt and, in reserve, at Bethune. This was near the northern edge of the old Somme battlefield, fought over in 1916 and again in 1918. It was a desolate area, subjected to a deliberate policy of total destruction by the enemy when they withdrew to the Hindenburg Line in 1917 and again during the withdrawals of the war's last year. Every tree, and every building had been 'removed from the face of the earth'. Prior to the Fourth Army attack near Amiens on August 8th the Battalion was very active with forward patrols and sniping between Le Hamel and Essars, rotating in front line and reserve with fellow battalions, the 1/6th South Staffs and the 8th Sherwood Foresters. This activity was designed to 'tie down' the German units while the set piece attack went in at Amiens. General Rawlinson and the Fourth Army enjoyed a notable success; Ludendorf, 'de facto' head of the German army, referred to it as the 'black day of the German army'.

This marked a change in the role of the BEF. Troops who had been accustomed to a stationary war now had to get used to a fluid situation with advances and retreats over open land. The Germans pursued tactics of pulling back, leaving highly-motivated and skilled machine gun squads behind who would take a heavy toll of infantry moving forward. Extensive mining and booby-traps added to the difficulties in advancing. The 1/6th Battalion entered the fray on September 28th, relieving the 1/5th South Staffs near the village of Bellenglise. Their advance brought heavy enemy resistance; casualties were caused by well-sited machine guns and shelling. Later in the day German counterattacks carried on for nearly six hours. The Battalion suffered heavy casualties; 'D' Company was practically surrounded and suffered grievous losses.

This was a situation where Bill Coltman would excel. By now he was beginning to enjoy a reputation among his fellow troops. Reputedly, he had sent a message back to his commanding officer, Lieutenant-Colonel Tomlinson, stating that he was too busy seeing to wounded than respond to an order to report to him. When his former C.O. died aged 81 he left £25 to Coltman in his will, 'the bravest man he ever met'. This fierce engagement would be the scene where Coltman would add a Bar to his DCM. In the new circumstances of 'open war' it should be appreciated that dangers had increased for the advancing troops. This period, known as 'the hundred days', was marked by an even greater level of casualties.

The citation clarifies the circumstances comprehensively and clearly:
'On the 28th September 1918, near Bellenglise, this NCO Stretcher-Bearer dressed and carried many wounded men under heavy artillery fire. During our advance on the following day he still remained at his work without rest or sleep, attending to the wounded, taking no heed of either shell or machine gun fire and never resting until he was positive that our sector was clear of wounded. In addition, he was a most valuable means of communication, bringing back with his wounded accurate information of the advance. In spite of the very thick smoke and fog he always found his way about and so far as his work allowed him he served as a guide. He set the very highest example of fearlessness and devotion to duty'.

This is a very detailed account of the reason for Coltman's award of a Bar to his Distinguished Conduct Medal. Besides the elements of devotion to duty when dealing with casualties, it is noticeable that his knowledge of the forward lines was used to inform higher authority of the situation out of sight of the senior officers. This was a war without radios where telephone lines were vulnerable to artillery fire and often were destroyed early in the battle. Up-to-date intelligence was vital to the appraisal and decision-making of the officers at headquarters, allowing them to move reserves or reinforce successful operations. This was an added role for Coltman and, with his knowledge of field craft, he was able to inform

65

commanders accurately and successfully. There can be little doubt that this aspect of his duty would help to save lives as much as his devoted work with the wounded.

Towards the end of his life Bill related to members of his family a little more about this incident. On the 28th he had been busy with others dressing and removing the wounded in the action which became known as the Battle of Bellenglise. The feature he recalled was the very heavy German artillery fire which they endured while getting casualties to safety. He had worked throughout the night without rest and when the next day dawned he was told about some wounded enemy soldiers who had been left during the allied advance. He decided that these men needed him and, although tired and under fire, he went forward and tended to their wounds. This is a notable recollection; Bill had no qualms about treating all in need, irrespective of their nationality. There can be little doubt that he found the parable of the Good Samaritan a lesson for his behaviour. How often, teaching his Sunday School pupils, would he have used this story to illustrate God's grace and mercy to those undeserving of it? In a practical way his behaviour would be an outworking of this. For all those casualties, lying out in 'No Man's Land', victims of 'man's hatred for his fellow man' Bill would become an angel of mercy to British or German; he would be the 'Samaritan' they needed.

This day, when Coltman treated these Germans in need, would be the most famous in the history of the 46th Division and the North Staffordshire Regiment. On the 29th September 1918 the Battalion was in support of the 4th Leicesters near to the St Quentin Canal. Using life belts (reputedly taken from cross-Channel transports) and scaling ladders they crossed the canal under fire and a group of men, commanded by Captain Charlton, found the bridge at Riqueval intact and crossed it, overpowering the defenders. They had 'broken the Hindenburg Line' in one of the most celebrated actions of the war. It was a monumental feat of arms, achieved at the relatively modest cost of 800 casualties. Bill's battalion had been fully involved, 150 casualties was their price but the mighty Siegfried Stellung had been breached – whatever was the truth about Gommecourt they were redeemed!

Bill Coltman's recollection of this fails to mention this great day in his unit's history – he was busy with German wounded!

Interestingly, this great achievement was to result in one of the most famous photographs of the Great War. Before sunset on that historic day the official British war photographer, David McClellan was present when Brigadier-General Campbell VC addressed the troops of the 46th on the almost vertical canal bank near to Riqueval Bridge. I write with this famous picture in front of me, some of the 'Tommies' still wearing the lifejackets referred to above. As Campbell addressed them from the bridge parapet, a pennant flutters above him. Who were these men? It is likely that one was a young man from Stafford, my wife's maternal grandfather, having recently joined the 1/6th after volunteering as a seventeen year old. Probably Lance-Corporal William Coltman DCM and Bar, MM and Bar was present – or was he still devoting his energies to those in need? One thing we do know; within a few days he would share Britain's highest award for valour with the general congratulating those men.

Crossing the Hindenburg Line did not mark the end. The open fighting which now ensued was some of the most costly of the whole war. In terms of daily casualties, units involved would suffer on a scale worse than even the bloodiest conflicts of the previous year. As the Germans had discovered in their Spring offensives, the attacking forces gain ground only at great cost when defenders show skill and resilience. The German army had both these qualities and there was 'no gain without pain'. On the 3rd October, after a spell of wet and cool weather, the battalion was attacking near to Levergies; their task was to capture a defensive feature known as the Fonsomme Line. Defended by few but skilful and determined soldiers using machine guns from well-prepared positions and supported by accurate pre-ranged artillery, the battalion took heavy casualties.

Within a few minutes of the morning attack commencing the Battalion Commander, Lieutenant-Colonel F. R. Evans, had been killed, Major C. C. Dowding DSO, detached from the King's Own Lancashire Regiment, taking charge. 'A' Company found themselves advancing by Mannequin Hill, near to the village of Sequehart. Later, Bill recalled that the first casualties had occurred as the men had formed up 'on the tapes' at 6.50am. These men were bandaged and sent back. There was heavy enemy fire as the battalion moved forward just after. Following an advance of about 250 metres, the forward elements came under withering machine gun fire and the shout of 'stretcher bearer' was heard. The teams moved forward to assist; as Bill went forward he recalled a soldier lying nearby, severely wounded. Before he could deal with him a bearer from the adjoining South Staffs battalion attended him. As he bent to treat him a large shell landed nearby and both were killed instantly.   By now the advance had moved on; the stretcher bearers combed the battlefield, checking for life, bandaging wounded and moving them back if possible. Casualties were so great that captured Germans returning to allied lines, were employed to carry back the stretcher cases. As darkness fell it became impossible to search for more and so the stretcher bearer teams returned to safer positions to rest and replenish their medical equipment.

As soon as dawn appeared, Coltman returned to his task. Now, the enemy, having had time to bring in reinforcements, counterattacked and the forward elements of the Division were forced to retire. In their haste, wounded men were left behind, exposed to enemy fire. By now he had earned a reputation for bravery second to none; leading the men to coin phrases such as 'If anyone can find you if you cop it; it'll be Billy. He don't get lost', or 'Don't worry, Bill'll get ya'. This was well earned, for seeing the wounded ahead, although the enemy fire was murderous, Coltman left cover on his own initiative and went forward to find and help the casualties in front. By now his situation was extremely perilous. The German machine gunners had managed to dig in on the flanks of the battle zone and the British front units were exposed to enfilade fire. Bill Coltman was alone, ahead of his own forces and exposed to enemy fire. Nevertheless he began to dress wounds and, when able, started to drag casualties back to cover, where he could pass them on to other bearers. Amazingly, three badly wounded comrades were found, bandaged and carried back by this bravest of men, placed over his shoulder in the 'fireman's lift' position. This was not unusual for Bill; he had taken men back like this many times under fire. Although only five feet four inches tall, his work on the land had helped to develop upper body strength and he was able to lift a man with relative ease. He continued to search the valley in the shadow of Mannequin Hill, recovering and treating the wounded until every casualty had been seen and tended to.

This remarkable feat had been witnessed by battalion officers. Acting Commanding Officer, Major Dowding had no doubts about recommending Coltman for the award of his country's highest medal for valour, the Victoria Cross.

The citation read:
'For most conspicuous bravery, initiative and devotion to duty. During the operations at Mannequin Hill, north-east of Sequehart, on the 3rd and 4th October 1918, Lance-Corporal Coltman, a stretcher bearer, hearing that wounded had been left behind during a retirement, on his own initiative went forward alone in the face of fierce enfilade fire, found the wounded, dressed them, and on three successive occasions carried comrades on his back to safety, thus saving their lives. This very gallant NCO tended the wounded unceasingly for 48 hours'.

This citation was published in the 'London Gazette' on January 6th 1919. By the time it was in the newspaper the war was over although Coltman was still with his unit in France. After what became known as the Battle of Beaurevoir the battalion spent time in action and in reserve during the months of October and November. Five days before the armistice came into operation they took part in a short but fierce attack near Le Sart, along the Beaurepaire-Prisches Road, in support of French forces. The casualties that day were the last suffered by 1/6th during the war.

On November 9th they relieved the 1/5th South Staffs in the line, but upon arrival their orders were changed and they marched back to billets in Fourmanoir. The next day the Brigade was paraded before Brigadier-General J. W. Campbell VC, CMG and DSO. During the medal parade, Coltman would have gone forward to display the ribbons of the DCM and MM. As yet the Victoria Cross award would not have been sanctioned. However, few men who knew him would have felt that he had not earned it many times over during the previous three years. Surely, Lance-Corporal William Harold Coltman's achievements can rank alongside those of Noel Chavasse VC and Bar from the Great War and Leonard Cheshire VC from the Second. For all three of these men the award of Britain's highest medal for valour reflected a devotion to duty unsurpassed in the twentieth century.

Chapter Seven

'Behold your king',
John chapter 19 verse 14

Today, with the benefit of hindsight, we know that the Great War effectively ended on the 11th November 1918. The soldiers at the front that day had no such awareness. Thankful that there had been a pause in proceedings, they knew it to be an armistice only, not an unconditional surrender. Ironically, perhaps tragically, the BEF found itself close to the town of Mons, where it had begun its journey in September 1914. Now, over four years later, the last British soldier was to be killed less than a mile from where the first had met his death; both lie near to each other in the beautiful cemetery at St. Symphonien near Mons, begun by the Germans in 1914.

The North Staffords were at Fourmanoir when the guns fell silent at 11am. The quiet must have been strange for men like Coltman who had endured over three years at the front. Few of the men of the BEF who had set off in August 1914 were there to witness this event – very few of the North Midland Territorial Division, who had landed in June 1915, were present; the human cost of Messines, Hill 60, Loos, Gommecourt, Bellenglise and Riqueval had been too great. Many were young volunteers and conscripts who had only been with the Division a few weeks, like George Mountford, my wife's grandfather who had lied about his age and reached the front in September – just in time to take part in the horrors of the 'last hundred days'.

For the survivors, the next few days spent in billets at Avensnes were a time of hope and of anxiety; hope that it was all over, anxiety that it might start again. The German army still remained in Belgium and France, no allied force had invaded 'the Fatherland'. Slowly, as pieces of information filtered through to the 'Tommies', it dawned on them that this titanic struggle was at an end. Some modern-day commentators point out the advantages for the future that would have lain in the allies continuing their attacks and invading Germany. This may have some validity, but it is hard to believe that these war-weary men who had been through so much in the previous few weeks could simply start it all over again after a temporary pause.

January 1919 saw the gazetting of William Coltman's VC. Although he had yet to receive the medal, the Brigade Medal Parade would have witnessed the formal announcement of the award; this taking place fittingly in France among his comrades he had worked so devotedly to protect.

On March 3rd, 1919 Lance-Corporal William Coltman, VC, DCM and Bar, MM and Bar was officially demobbed from His Majesty's Armed Forces, over four years after he had enlisted. He returned to his home in Forest Road; it is probable that he had spent less than a month there in the previous four years. It is hard for us to imagine what it must have been like for a returning husband and father at that time. No surviving record of Bill's homecoming exists. However, my mother, born in June 1914 and a similar age to Bill's son Charles, recalled the return of her father from that war by stating that she hid from him when he arrived. Not only had she no idea who he was, she had lived the first four years of her life in a completely female household with her grandma, mum and two older sisters as companions – there were few men around!

Whatever Bill Coltman's homecoming was like we can be certain that he would have hurried along to the first gathering of his brethren and sisters at the converted granary in Winshill, his spiritual home. On the first Sunday, or 'Lord's Day' as he would have referred to it, Bill would have sat among the Fellowship involved in silent and audible prayer. When the time came for the bread and wine to be taken in memory of his risen Lord he would have remembered that Jesus had died to purchase his freedom from the power of sin in his life. God had preserved him through the horror of the trenches in order that he might be able to show the presence of his Lord in his life. He might have recalled the 'Calvarys' that had been a feature of the French countryside, many damaged by the indiscriminate shelling that had so blighted the land. Bill had 'borne his cross' in that foreign land where his actions had preached 'the cross and Christ crucified' more eloquently than words or roadside shrines ever could. For so many returning soldiers adapting to civilian life would prove to be enormously difficult; minds constantly going back to the horrors of the war. For Bill that element of his life was now consigned to the past – now he would seek to live for his Lord in Burton-upon-Trent just as he had done in northern France.

We might assume that the most decorated NCO of the war would return to great acclaim and a choice of employment. But this was 1919, in the aftermath of a national catastrophe. After the initial celebrations the mood became sombre. The full impact of over a million dead and twice that number wounded began to 'sink in'. As the bunting became faded, it was beggars and match sellers that decorated the streets, a constant reminder of the 'land fit for heroes' to which these 'heroes' had returned. Fittingly, for a man of his character, Bill Coltman returned quietly to work at the home of Colonel C. J. Goer in Ashby Road, Burton as a gardener, the job he had left in 1915 to enlist.

However, on the 21st May he travelled to London for a very important appointment. With his brother George, he reported to Wellington Barracks, and then spent the rest of the day touring the sights of the capital. Next day they set off to Buckingham Palace and there, on a warm spring day, he paraded with two other VC winners, George Kerr and Bellenden Hucheson in the Palace Quadrangle. Kerr would receive the VC and MC on the same day, all three men would be decorated with the nation's highest award for bravery, a small Maltese cross, made from a bronze Russian cannon barrel captured at Sebastopol during the Crimean War. Bearing the motto 'For Valour' it entitled him to wear the crimson ribbon which denoted the ultimate in gallantry and devotion to duty, only given to those who had risked 'the jaws of death'. Coltman never forgot the words of His Majesty, 'Yours is one of the very few, if not the only case in the whole British army, where a man has gained so many distinctions. I heartily congratulate you'.

All this and he had never fired a shot in anger!

An interesting anecdote about this event gives us an insight into Coltman's character and how he regarded the award. Before returning by train to Burton with his brother George, he became aware that it was the intention of some of the civic leaders and dignitaries of the town to provide a reception at the railway station. A man who respected others but abhorred fuss, Bill left the train at the station prior to the town and walked home. He saw no reason to indulge in 'back-slapping'. He had received the due reward for what he had done, that was enough. Many years later, when he was an overseer at the Meeting Room in Winshill, the question of a suitable colour arose for the interior painting of the building.   Deciding on a new scheme was causing a problem so Bill went down to the Hall at 4am and proceeded to paint it the colour he wanted. The discussion ceased and the building had been repainted. It was in the nature of the man that he had little time for debate; the most important thing was to get the job done!

The year 1920 saw Bill back in London at least twice more. On the 26th of June he accepted an invitation to attend King George V's Garden Party at Buckingham Palace to honour all the surviving winners of the VC. Although Bill rarely gave interviews or attended military functions, he attended the regular VC winners' meetings and royal functions. Later in the year, he would be called upon to witness one of the most moving and singular events of the immediate post war period.

It is very difficult for us today to appreciate the effect that the losses of the Great War had on the British people. Figures for the total death toll for the United Kingdom and her Dominions and Empire are difficult to ascertain but it is accepted that total military deaths exceeded one million, one hundred thousand. Over 800,000 of those were from Britain alone. Never before, or since, has this country suffered to that degree. Worst of all, over a quarter of a million of the dead had no grave. Some means had to be found to allow those who had lost loved ones to be able to mourn. Over the next fifteen years the work of the Imperial (now the Commonwealth) War Graves Commission would seek, through cemeteries abroad and building memorials to the missing in Belgium and France, to remember appropriately the 720,000 dead and missing of the Western Front. Today, this work continues; amazingly, British soldiers' remains are still unearthed in the fields of France and Belgium, over ninety years after their death.

Many grieving families found it impossible to travel over to the Continent, although organizations began to provide the first 'package holidays' to enable working-class people to visit the grave or memorial associated with their loss. As a means of meeting the needs of those who could not visit, or had no grave to travel to, it was decided that a temporary memorial would be placed in Whitehall as a focus for national mourning. The architect Edward Lutyens had been given a commission to build a suitable memorial, to be a central feature of the Victory Celebrations planned for July 19th. What emerged was a cenotaph or empty tomb of simple non-religious design, hurriedly constructed out of wood and plaster in a few days; it was a large sarcophagus; just three words emblazoned it: 'The Glorious Dead'.

The crowds of people drawn to the Victory Celebration from all over Britain and beyond turned this temporary monument into what was tantamount to a shrine. Mountains of flowers surrounded it; many were moved elsewhere to allow road access. The national response was so great that it was clear that this temporary structure would have to be replaced by a permanent cenotaph. This was arranged and its dedication was planned for November 11th 1920 when the remembrance would involve the burial of 'an unknown warrior' in Westminster Abbey, a fitting resting place among the Kings and Queens of England. On a misty November morning, a Royal Navy destroyer crossed the Channel, escorted by French warships. It bore the remains of a British soldier whose body had been found somewhere in France or Belgium and was unable to be identified.

This 'unknown warrior', as he became known, would be taken to London, the cortege bearing his body passing the Cenotaph in Whitehall and ending its journey at the Abbey where he would be interred just inside the entrance. To line the last few metres to its final resting place the most decorated servicemen from the three branches of the armed forces had been chosen; among them was the stretcher bearer from Burton on Trent. These chosen men were honorary pall-bearers to the warrior who would stand for all those lost in the war and having no known grave. One wonders about his thoughts as this cortege passed by. How did Bill Coltman feel, wearing the medals he had won with distinction, as he filed past the coffin in Westminster Abbey after the Service of Remembrance had come to a close? Those who had lived paid their respects to the one who had paid the ultimate price – it mirrored the Christian gospel which had such a special meaning for Bill.

Life in Burton returned to 'normal' for the Coltman family, soon to be blessed with a daughter, Dorothy. In 1922 a major event for the family occurred when the Granary used for eighteen years as a meeting house was replaced with a building in North Street, Winshill. Now this group of believers had a building of their own; Bill cheerfully contributed to it, both financially and with physical help. He would attend the gatherings there for the rest of his life. The Gospel Hall at North Street no longer stands. It was demolished as part of a local development and the 'Brethren' Assembly provided with a new building which is used today.

Chapter Eight

'Serving God day and night',
Acts chapter 26 verse 7

The 1920s and 30s were times when most people chose to forget about the war. Robert Graves' autobiographical record *Goodbye to All That* gives a contemporary and accurate picture of the outlook of the day, including a rather amusing reference to the Irish 'Plymouth Brethren' in Limerick. Certainly the lifestyle of Bill and his family would seem unusual today, with their strict teetotal attitude and the avoidance of entertainment like the radio, cinema and theatre. Their life would revolve around the outworking of Christian scriptural teaching and principles; a sober life which would demand modesty in dress and behaviour, hard work and devotion to and attendance at the Meeting Room. As in all matters the Bible, or word of God as Bill and his family would refer to it, would be the final arbiter in all questions of behaviour – would this honour our Lord a frequently asked question.

Caught up in his spiritual and family life, and working long hours (but never Sundays!) for first Colonel Goer and then Burton Parks and Gardens Department, Bill still found time to attend the special events arranged for holders of the Victoria Cross. In 1922 the second memorial to his old division was unveiled at Bellenglise, not far from where he had won the last two of his medals for gallantry. He could not attend and, as far as is known, never travelled back to the scene of his achievements – there was too much to do at home with the Meeting Room and his family demanding his attention. He did find time to attend the ceremony at Whittington Barracks near Lichfield, where two memorials to the North and South Staffordshire Regiments were unveiled; no one knows what he thought of them, one dragon and the other a sphinx surmounting stone obelisks.

In 1929 the Prince of Wales, later the uncrowned King Edward the Eighth, visited Burton-upon-Trent and, as the town's leading wartime figure, Bill was introduced to him. Reputedly, they conversed with each other for a short time and shook hands. The Prince had visited the trenches on a number of occasions and, like another modern-day Prince, had wished to become 'one of the men'. This had been prevented but, as a person and as Colonel-in-Chief of the Regiment, he took a lively interest in the old 'Tommies' he had so respected. One feels that, although divided by social and educational standing, the two men had much in common; fierce loyalty and a dislike of pointless talk and showmanship. Later in the year, on November 8th, Bill travelled to London again, meeting the Prince at a special dinner at the House of Lords prior to the annual Remembrance Parade.

By now the mood of the country was turning against war. After all, people had been led to believe that this was 'the war to end wars'. How could the appalling sacrifice of a generation be justified if it did not lead to a brave new world with a safer life for all? In 1929, Adolf Hitler was an unknown figure to most British people. Strangely, Coltman and Hitler shared the distinctions of having served on the Western front, been awarded medals for bravery and never being wounded save for the effects of gas. It was there that their paths diverged; for the Austrian painter war had provided him with the best days of his life – for the Burton gardener it was a terrible waste, an indictment of men for their sin and hatred. While Hitler remembered his war with affection, Bill Coltman would state in a 1960 *Daily Express* interview, 'I don't believe in guns and war'.

The 1930s witnessed the growth of the Nazi Party in Germany and its re-emergence as an aggressive militaristic power. On September 3rd 1939 Britain again declared war on Germany; it was a Sunday morning when the news broke. There could be no doubt where Bill was – meeting with his family and fellow Christians in the North Street Meeting Room. Perhaps, like a late friend of mine from Warrington, he left such a gathering to hear the announcement in the street as he made his way home. Once again Britain would be plunged into a titanic struggle; again, Christians would wrestle with their consciences over what was right for them to do.

Bill was in his forty-eighth year when the Second World War commenced. He was too old to be called back to the armed forces. However, he had no doubt that he must serve his country again. He joined the Special Constabulary until the local army depot in Burton realized that his ability was being somewhat wasted and he was asked to take command of the Burton Cadet Force with the rank of Captain. So it was that he would again answer his country's call. Still fit and active, he would be seen walking briskly around the depot, beret at a slight angle and sometimes with a 'swagger stick' under his arm. By now he needed glasses and these, together with a moustache and deep riveting blue eyes, made him a distinctive character. Just over five years ago, in a local supermarket, I met a veteran of the North Staffordshires selling poppies. An opportunity to have a conversation with a 'vet' should never be missed and so I enquired about his service. He told me that he had just been too young to see active service in the Second World War but had served in Korea. When I asked him if he knew of the subject of this story his eyes sparkled and he almost came to attention as he spoke. To him, as a young recruit in 1945 Bill was Captain Coltman; he went on to relate that he had seen him on many occasions and noticed the crimson ribbon on his chest. Enquiring about it, he had been told that this middle-aged, rather bulldog-looking man was the most famous VC winner in the Regiment's history. To some of the men he was known as 'Bill of Burton'.

After the end of the war Bill Coltman attended the Victory Parade on the eighth of June 1946. He marched in the VC Parade during the Centenary Review in Hyde Park ten years later before attending a special dinner hosted by H. M. The Queen in Buckingham Palace on the 27th of June, a Thanksgiving Service in Westminster Abbey and a Garden Party at Marlborough House. Later he had tea with the Queen at Windsor Castle. The VC anniversary celebrations were a special pleasure for him; the opportunity to meet fellow holders and dine in the presence of the Monarch or senior Royal figures. The following year he was again introduced to Her Majesty during a Royal visit to Burton and he met other senior Royal personages, including the Duke of Edinburgh, Princess Margaret and the Duke of

Gloucester. In June 1961 Bill was invited to attend the VC Reunion in London, which included Dinner at the Mansion House and a garden party at Buckingham Palace. He was allowed two guests to attend with him and chose to take his oldest grandson, John and oldest granddaughter, Barbara.

John described his emotions as they attended the Royal Garden Party. It appeared that those invited mingled in the garden of the Palace and then Royal equerries approached selected guests and invited them to meet Her Majesty. Imagine the incredulous faces of his grandchildren as Bill was informed of the opportunity to meet the Monarch. John remembers his growing excitement at the thought of meeting no less a person than Queen Elizabeth II. Then he recalls his disappointment at his grandfather's reply, 'Let someone else have the opportunity to meet the Queen: I've met her many times. After all I'm in contact daily with the King of kings'. Recollection of lines from Kipling's poem 'If' spring to mind here. For Bill, all were equal in the sight of God.

In his later years, Bill began to be a little more forthcoming about his wartime experiences. In February 1960 he was interviewed by leading presenter Cliff Michelmore on the BBC TV programme *Tonight*, a surprising decision to appear by a man who had once fled through the back door of his home when a local TV crew appeared at the front. In the same year he gave a newspaper interview to the *Sunday Express* where he talked about the remarkable bequest in Colonel Tomlinson's will. Despite his late C.O.'s recorded admiration for his bravery, Coltman suggested that it might have been left in token of his 'insubordination' when he had refused to report to guide a visiting officer around because he had a wounded man 'who needed him more'. On a more serious note, he did make his views about fighting known, explaining that it was his sincere hope that no one would ever win a VC again because there would be no opportunity to do so. As an elder or overseer at the North Street Meeting, Sunday School Superintendent and committed Christian above all else, he had an abhorrence of war and the death and suffering it caused.

The decade of the 1960s saw a re-awakening of media interest in the Great War. The previous twenty years had been dominated by cinema and TV recollections and reconstructions of the last one. Now, as the veterans of 1914-18 began to pass away, attempts were made to record their reminiscences. This media interest was epitomised in the 26-part BBC series *The Great War* where the remarkable film extracts were combined with fresh, new appraisals and personal memories. The public began to realize that the earlier conflict had not just been a pointless exercise in carnage but a conflict dominated by the mass mobilization of men and material. Perhaps the ten million dead had not died in vain after all. The national awakening resulted in much greater prominence being given to the surviving 'vets' and, in 1962, the town of Burton-upon-Trent decided to do something tangible to celebrate its most famous 'old soldier'.

Chapter Nine

'Honour the face of the old man',
Leviticus chapter 19 verse 32

The idea of the town of Burton-upon-Trent paying tribute to William Coltman arose during a council meeting in 1962. Bill's health had deteriorated; he would require a major operation and had decided to retire in a few months time. He had been a gardener all his life, except for the war years, and, latterly, had looked after the Wheatley Recreation Ground near to his home. Councillor Caulton raised the matter of providing a permanent tribute to Bill in the Town Hall. Not only had he been one of the town's most distinguished citizens, he had also worked for the Corporation (later Council) Parks Department for over twenty-five years. After discussion, it was decided to honour him by placing his photograph in the Mayor's Parlour. This would be a copy of a portrait, an oil painting by Mr. A. R. Todd, begun not long after the Victoria Cross had been won. Alongside would be his citations for bravery and, temporarily, a display of his medals between the Regimental Colours.

On a bitterly cold Thursday, February 21st, 1963 Bill Coltman was removing overnight snow from the Recreation Ground when he walked home, changed his clothes and travelled the short distance to the Town Hall in Burton. There, members of his family, close personal associates, and colleagues from the Staffordshire Regiment had gathered with Councillors and other Civic dignitaries for the official unveiling of the photograph. Bill was 73 years old; a newspaper photograph taken at his home had showed him looking rather tired and ill besides the original portrait of himself fourty-four years previously. Although the hair was greyer and spectacles hid his eyes, it was the same man in spirit and in attitude. At the Reception in the Council Chamber, the photograph was unveiled officially by the Mayor, Alderman G. T. Osborne. After the ceremony of acceptance, Lieutenant-Colonel Baines, C.O. of the 5/6th Battalion North Staffordshire Regiment T.A. said in his speech that

83

Coltman was 'No ordinary man, he had an enviable record which has never been equalled. It is a truly magnificent achievement'.

The last speaker was Colonel John Jackson, the Colonel of the North Staffs Regiment. He ended by saying, 'Mr Coltman will not be Lance-Corporal Coltman VC, DCM and Bar, MM and Bar but will be known as "Bill of Burton"'.

Bill's approach to these events when interviewed was typical, 'They didn't make so much fuss in the old days. It was a real surprise when I received the Mayor's invitation. It will be something of an ordeal'.

As the room cleared at the end of the reception, his hard-earned medals were placed on a table; the regimental drums and colours standing by them attested to the old warrior who had fought his fight and brought honour to his town and his comrades.

Bill, however, had not fought his last fight. After winning the battle against ill-health he was to take up two other causes close to his heart. In his last years 'in this scene' he would show the dogged determination that had marked an earlier path.

Retirement from Council employment allowed Bill to indulge his passion for the countryside. He enjoyed bee-keeping; some of his grandchildren's earliest memories are of his tending the bee hives at the rear of his extensive garden in Wheatley Lane. There he lived quietly with his daughter Dorothy, her husband Alan and their daughter Barbara. They had moved into his home after the tragic loss of his dear wife Eleanor. On Christmas Eve 1948 she had succumbed to cancer, the day before Christ's birth would be remembered. As people celebrated God's coming from heaven to earth, Bill faced the reality that his wife had passed from earth to heaven. While his family looked to care for him, he had the time to look after his allotments with the same devotion and care he had always shown. Often he would walk over the nearby hills to Bretby, a man who enjoyed being close to the nature. In his later years, he bought a television; indeed, grandson John's only memory of his mentioning the VC was when he commented that his annual pension had been increased during a Budget Day announcement! He never spoke about the war to friends or family but meticulously kept the invitations he received to special events, travelling to them in his son-in-law's car.

In 1968 a special anniversary Parade of the Staffordshire Regiment took place on 'Arnhem Day' in September. The two Regimental VC winners of World War Two had both earned their awards in that famous encounter at 'a bridge too far'. While Lance-Sergeant Baskeyfield had died there, the other recipient, Major Richard Caine, was alongside the 76 year old veteran as they took the salute of the parading 1st North Staffords as they marched to Lichfield Cathedral. Outside the Guild Hall the Mayor, Councillor G. W. Deacon stood between the two honoured guests on the saluting base, both men removing their bowler hats in tribute to their modern-day comrades. It was fitting that the Parade had also commemorated the Battle of the St. Quentin Canal of 1918, fifty years before. A service led by the Rev. W. Macpherson followed; old comrades from the 'Terriers' were present but Bill must have been aware that their numbers were dwindling.

William Coltman's attendance at events like this testified to his strong links with his old comrades and fellow VC winners. His respect for the institutions and agencies in society was in contrast to his dislike of many of the modern trends. He linked the recent increase in vandalism with the end of National Service. In 1972 he gave another newspaper interview to air his views about this. In it he lamented the lack of control over young people at home and in school and the associated vandalism which was blighting society. To an old soldier of eighty-one he could neither tolerate nor understand these developments. The Bible taught strictly regarding the proper raising of children – 'spare the rod and spoil the child' would have echoed his outlook. After complaining about this lack of discipline he went on to suggest that the army would be able to instil the necessary discipline and respect in the lives of contemporary youth. Some years before, he had confronted a group of 'teddy boys' bent on vandalising the Wheatley Recreation Ground. When one of their number recognized him, they left the scene at his request. Perhaps they linked the VC with bravery and killing; in Bill's case they were half right! The day after he had given the interview, he attended a reception at the Mayor's Parlour for the last time.

As a deeply committed Christian man William Coltman knew and believed that death came to all, if His risen Saviour should choose to wait to return. For Bill, when a person died was less important than the eternal state which they passed into. He had witnessed death more than most; death in so many ways as a result of man's hatred of his fellow-man. The most important thing was how a man had prepared for that death. When Bill was taken ill in the spring of 1974, it was, nevertheless, a surprise; up to a few weeks before he had been enjoying his hobbies and pastimes in his modest semi-detached house in Wheatley Lane. He had began to suffer from a form of dementia, possibly Lewy Body dementia which causes visual hallucination and unsteadiness in walking. After a short stay in hospital he passed away quietly in Outlands Hospital on 29th June 1974, aged 83. Shortly before he had 'gone home to be with His Lord' he had said, 'I sincerely hope that future generations will know nothing of war – only what they read in books – and never again will there come a time when a Victoria Cross can be won'.

Chapter Ten

'Into thy resting place',
2 Chronicles chapter 6 verse 41

When William Coltman's coffin passed through the streets of Winshill on the afternoon of Thursday, July 4th 1974 no less than twelve awards graced it. They are listed below:

The Victoria Cross
The Distinguished Conduct Medal and Bar
The Military Medal and Bar
The 1915 Campaign Medal
The 1914-18 War Medal
The 1918 Victory Medal with oak leaf
Defence Medal
King George VI Coronation Medal
Special Constabulary Medal
Queen Elizabeth II Coronation Medal

The twelve awards (10 medals, 2 Bars) are listed for information purposes. Bill would have been the last man to 'glory' in them. Yet they exemplify a life of service for his fellow men and for his nation. They testify to a devoted life – and yet the most important element of it would only now become a reality.

The funeral service took place at North Street Meeting Room commencing at 2.30pm. In keeping with the lay traditions of the 'Brethren' it was conducted by Mr J. Hinks. Opportunity was given for the family, friends and over one hundred gathered outside in the pouring rain, to hear the service by means of loudspeakers. Fittingly, a plain coffin containing Bill's mortal remains was placed in the small Hall which he had co-founded fifty-two years before. Some may have felt the Parish Church or even Lichfield Cathedral to have been a more fitting venue, but this place was treasured in his heart and totally fitting for a man who had lived without pomp or fame. The plain, simple surroundings of this building which he had helped to construct fitted the straightforward nature of the man. During the service the gospel message was clearly presented. Bill would have wanted that; for over sixty years of his life His Saviour and God had meant more to him than anything – even the members of his family who mourned his passing. The order of service simply spoke of his being 'Called Home' on the previous Saturday. In keeping with the simplicity of this part of the proceedings, the printed words were simple yet profound: 'Rest in the Lord'.

Afterwards, the funeral cortege moved into the streets of his home, Winshill; the coffin now adorned with a Union Flag and a mass of floral tributes. The procession, soldiers with rifles reversed, made its way slowly from the Hall to the nearby church where the military honours would be carried out in the Churchyard. As Mr Hinks and the Rev. R. Cheadle, Regimental Chaplain, led the way a guard of honour was formed by the Mercian Volunteers, and the Regimental Depot Band paid tribute in music, including the slow march *God Bless The Prince of Wales*. A solitary bugler played the *Last Post*. In front of many local dignitaries, military representatives and old comrades who had travelled from far and wide, William Harold Coltman was laid to rest in the grave of his dear wife Eleanor who had preceded his 'calling home' in 1948.

Some newspaper reports afterwards commented that a volley of three shots was fired over the grave in tribute to a man who had never fired one himself in anger. The irony of this would not have been lost on Bill! Today, a simple grey stone grave stands at the back of the churchyard, tended by local school pupils and looked after by the Mercian Regiment. Few local people visit; most are probably not even aware of it.

On the 21st May, 1977 at 3.00pm a Memorial to Bill was dedicated in the square in front of the Burton Technical College. A plaque was unveiled by the Lord Lieutenant of the County, Sir Arthur Bryan. In front of family, friends, civic officials, military representatives and a crowd of over 200, Sir Arthur said, 'There have been few instances of such bravery as that shown by Captain Coltman from the time he was first mentioned in despatches on the Somme until he earned the Victoria Cross'. The Memorial was dedicated by the Reverend R. Cheadle and, afterwards, the 1st battalion of the Staffordshire Regiment under the command of Major H. G. Willmore marched through the town to the drill hall. Survivors from the 1/6th were fittingly present, including over 200 veterans from the British Legion. The Memorial had been funded by donations from many associated with the old Territorial Battalion.

On the death of his son Charles, Bill's medal collection was passed on to the Regiment he had served and today (2008) the Barracks and Museum at Whittington, near to Lichfield, displays 'The Coltman Trench', a replica of one from the First World War, a feature of Bill's service. It is fitting to close this narrative by wondering how many men were brought safely back to the relative safety of the trenches by this brave stretcher bearer from Burton.

The words on the memorial plaque to Bill Coltman in Burton-upon-Trent:

CAPTAIN WILLIAM HAROLD COLTMAN VC DCM MM

A DISTINGUISHED CITIZEN OF BURTON UPON TRENT AND OF STAFFORDSHIRE, WHO AS A LANCE CORPORAL IN THE 1st/6th BATTALION, THE NORTH STAFFORDSHIRE REGIMENT (THE PRINCE OF WALES'S) WAS AWARDED THE VICTORIA CROSS, THE DISTINGUISHED CONDUCT MEDAL AND BAR, AND THE MILITARY MEDAL AND BAR, AND WAS ALSO MENTIONED IN DESPATCHES FOR HIS WORK AS AN UNARMED STRETCHER BEARER IN FRANCE DURING THE 1914-18 WAR.

BORN 17.11.1891   DIED 29.6.1974

Conclusions

'Thou good and faithful servant',
Matthew chapter 25 verse 21

I never met William Coltman and I have never been involved in a war. What I do know is based on historical research, the statements of people who were acquainted with him and my 'inside' knowledge of the 'Brethren'. Additionally, reading about the war, and frequent visits to the Western front area have helped to give some background to this account.

Despite the obvious drawbacks of never meeting the subject himself, over sixteen years of considering his personality, conversations, anecdotes and research into the life of this remarkable Christian man has led to two clear words to describe him fittingly: **single-minded devotion**.

These two adjectives sum up Bill Coltman. In one way he was a product of his times; a period when the qualities he personified were not ridiculed as they are today. Whatever Bill did he applied the same degree of devotion to it as well as a determination to focus on the task until it was done – and done properly. In the era of 'taking a sicky', we are surprised that, whether serving his Lord, caring for his family, tending the ground or rescuing wounded comrades (and enemies) he approached each one the same way: to do it to the best of his ability.

In the decade before his death it became fashionable to be something of a maverick figure. It was suggested that Bill's refusal to attend his C.O. was indicative of this. This is far from the truth. This incident gives us an insight into the man. He was not being insubordinate; he had a more important matter to attend to: a man in need! In Bill's eyes, this was far more important than showing a visiting officer around. Years later when he chose not to meet H. M. The Queen it was not a mark of disrespect; his answer reflected the reality; he had been introduced to her on many previous occasions. He would have read in the Bible that he should 'Honour all men. Love the brotherhood. Fear God. Honour the King'. He was never concerned with reputation, fame or medals for the sake of them. His awards were earned; the due reward for his deeds. However, he lived his life with the constant awareness that God had rewarded him in spite of his deeds.

William Coltman VC never did anything to earn eternal life except to put his complete trust in his Lord and Saviour, Jesus Christ, who had died for him on the cross of Calvary. This act of sacrifice had been sufficient to meet the demands of God the Father in bringing about redemption for the wrongdoer. Nothing Bill did could add to that price which had been paid almost 2000 years previously. What he could do was serve his God, his country and his comrades in the most dedicated way, by doing everything to the best of his ability. Each citation emphasizes this aspect, an untiring effort to serve.

Asked once why he had opted for the role of a Regimental stretcher bearer in 1915, he answered that it was because he felt it to be a 'soft job'. This was not the true reason, as palpably it was not, and he knew it. In truth, being a stretcher bearer allowed him to reconcile two conflicting issues in his life – devotion and service. He could serve his nation and comrades while remaining devoted to the word of God which was 'a lamp unto my feet and a light unto my path'.[6]

As a member of the 'Brethren' for many years before the war, Bill could have sought, and probably claimed, exemption from military service on the basis of conscience. Recently, in a telephone conversation with a Television programme producer, I was asked if I considered Coltman to have been a conscientious objector. My answer was that, although he was always driven by his personal conscience before God, he rarely objected to what he was asked to do. It is noticeable that he acted as a means of communication and

---

6 Quoted from Psalm 119 verse 105. Quoted from the New King James Version of the Bible.

carried out reconnaissance which were not strictly the roles demanded of a non-combatant. He would willingly accept the dangers, privations and suffering of the trenches without objecting. All this was consistent with his beliefs, but the killing of another contravened the scriptural truths which governed his life.

The decision facing the committed Christian in 1914 was a difficult one. For the first time in recent history Britain faced a peril which demanded the involvement of all in society. If this was not apparent straightaway, it dawned on the population by the end of the year when most of the 'Old Contemptibles' were dead, or back in 'Blighty'. The 'Brethren' were, and are, a group known for their strict adherence to scriptural truths. Bill Coltman would have been very aware of the account in Matthew's Gospel when the priests brought a penny to the Lord Jesus; His answer that they should, 'Render therefore unto Caesar the things which are Caesar's and unto God the things that are God's'[7] would have confirmed him in his desire to serve his nation but honour God before all men. He could satisfy the requirements of 'today' whilst not compromising his future integrity before his Lord. It must always be remembered that Coltman volunteered for the army over a year before he would have been conscripted; working on the land, it is possible that he could have then claimed 'reserved occupation status' and never been asked to serve. Whatever were the reasons, the rightness of the cause, the desire to serve his nation, we shall never know. However, the fact that he arrived at the Recruiting Office in Burton on a cold morning in January tells us that he had a clear desire to 'do his bit' for the war effort.

Today William Coltman VC is honoured by his old regiment and by his childhood town. The house where he lived over the last twenty years of his life 'in this scene' is still called *Sequehart* and a small Victoria Cross accompanies the name. Together with that of Baskeyfield VC, his medals were dedicated in 2007 at a ceremony in

---

[7] Quoted from Matthew chapter 22 verse 21. Quoted from the King James Version of the Bible.

Lichfield Cathedral. Left in his will to his son, they were to be passed on to the Staffordshire Regiment after Charles' death. Bill was a pragmatist; by the time he died, he was aware that he had two grandsons, both bearing the family name. As usual he sought an honourable and fair way of dealing with this. Their value today is estimated to be over £200,000 as a set. This would never have interested Bill. He did not ignore them, or not value them; a miniature set sit in the living room of his old home today, but he did not lay great store on earthly goods. He never owned a car or any of the modern trappings of a comfortable life. He sought to 'lay up treasures . . . in heaven' rather than those of earth which would become corrupted.[8]

The Victoria Cross has been awarded over a thousand times since it was instituted by the Queen whose name it bears over 120 years ago. The men who have received it have a variety of stories to tell. Some, like fellow North Staffordshire winner John Baskeyfield, died in the act, his body never recovered. Today, a large statue stands in the Festival Park, near Hanley, and a nearby school bears his name; visiting Arnhem today, the scene of his heroism, a plaque stands marking the spot where he fell. Outside his 'home' town there is no memorial to Bill, but his name graces the trench display at the Regimental Museum, the depot in Burton is called 'Coltman House', and a road in Sandyford, Stoke-on-Trent bears his name in full. The year 2008 has seen the Battlefield Tour specialists 'Leger Holidays' include a visit to Sequehart in one of their tour itineraries. Why then are his medals worth so much today?

The answer lies in the circumstances in which they were won. Some men won the VC when they carried out a single act of amazing bravery. Often out of character, they acted in 'the heat of battle' and, if surviving, probably wondered afterwards why they had done it! Some became enraged by what they had witnessed and, in a haze, carried out the act for which they are remembered. Some like

---

8 Quoted from Matthew chapter 6 verse 20. The full account covers verses 19-21. Quoted from the New King James Version of the Bible.

Chavasse, Cheshire, and Coltman carved their name into history because they saw it as their duty; serving their country and their God. This is an old-fashioned concept today, but it does not diminish their achievements. These men, and others, faced up to the realities of what they were doing. When they won their awards, both men had served at the front over a long period and were fully aware of the dangers involved in exposure to enemy fire. They had time to consider the risk involved. It was not done to win medals; all would have dismissed that notion. It was done out of devotion to duty. By the grave of Noel Chavasse, my thoughts turned to Bill Coltman. Both are now dead, in far different circumstances from each other; what they shared was the desire to use their ability to the uttermost to save others in need. This is the essence of the Christian gospel. We have a saying that 'actions speak louder than words'. Bill Coltman was, in a very special way, proclaiming Christ, not by what he said – more by what he did. The apostle James reminds us that 'faith without works' is meaningless.[9]

If the Great War had not taken place at the time when Bill Coltman was old enough to serve, his name would be known to very few today, except his family. He would have lived out his life quietly as a gardener in Burton-upon-Trent, serving his community, caring for his family and attending a place of worship regularly. None of these are very remarkable in themselves, but history is littered with 'ordinary people' who, when called to serve, do 'the extraordinary'. William Coltman, VC, DCM and Bar, MM and Bar is a prime example of such a person. If he had not travelled to France in 1915 and been caught up in the most terrible of wars, he would have devoted himself to his life at home with the same degree of devotion and commitment. Wartime service was an extension of his approach to life, governed by the principles that he was 'to serve God' in all aspects of his life. The prophet Isaiah in the first chapter of his book in the Old Testament writes these words:
'From the sole of the foot even to the head there is no soundness in

---

[9] Quoted from James chapter 2 verse 26. Quoted from the King James Version of the Bible.

it; but wounds, and bruises, and putrefying sores: they have not been closed, or bound up, or soothed with ointment. Your country is desolate. Your cities are burned with fire; strangers devour your land in your presence; and it is desolate, as overthrown by strangers'.[10]

What a vivid picture of the battleground which Coltman knew so well! Consider how, in the aftermath of that conflict, his thoughts would have been taken back to that horrific scene when he opened his Bible at that passage. And yet he never spoke to his family or friends about it; he never wrote down any of his experiences; he did not appear to ever dream or have nightmares about what he had witnessed. This is extraordinary. Even in his final illness, none of the hallucinations which affected him were rooted in wartime experiences.

To understand this, we must seek to understand the man. William Coltman was a simple man. That is not meant as a criticism; in the present over-complicated world we live in, it is intended as a compliment. He was able to cut through the unimportant elements of life and identify the most vital – health, family, service but most of all faith. When he worked in his allotments towards the end of his life, he applied the same devotion as he did in everything else. Confident that his eternal life was in the hands of the Almighty, he sought not to earn salvation but to hear those words, 'Well done, thou good and faithful servant: thou hast been faithful over a few things, I will make thee ruler over many things: enter thou into the joy of thy lord'.[11]

Today, while the awards he earned remain here on earth, Bill Coltman is in the enjoyment of the heavenly rewards his Lord earned for him. Which is the more important, the cross of Victoria or the cross of Calvary? Bill Coltman knew the answer!

---

[10] Quoted from Isaiah chapter 6 verses 6-7. Quoted from the New King James Version of the Bible.

[11] Quoted from Matthew chapter 25 verse 21. Quoted from the King James Version of the Bible.

Bibliography

To list all the books I have read concerning the Western front would take several pages; these below are ones which I have consulted in the preparation of this account of Bill Coltman's life.

GAVIN STAMP, *The Memorial to the Missing of the Somme*, Profile Books, 2006

MARTIN MIDDLEBROOK, *The North Midland Territorials Go to War*, Leo Cooper, 2003

GERALD GLIDDON, *The Final Days 1918 (VCs of the 1st World War)*, Sutton Publishing, 2000

FRASER SKIRROW, *Massacre on the Marne*, Pen and Sword, 2007

K. W. MITCHINSON, *Riqueval (Battleground Europe Series)*, Leo Cooper, 1998

The Bible – King James Version, Oxford University Press

The Bible – New King James Version, Thomas Nelson Publishers, 1994

The Bible – New International Version, International Bible Society, 1973

The School Bill attended at Rangemore

THE COLTMAN TRENCH

Coltman World War I Trench Display, Whittington

Special Constable Burton 1940

Bill's birthplace in Rangemore today (2008)

William Coltman VC at a V.C. Reunion c.1961

The medal collection - now held by the Mercian Regiment

Tribute at the National Memorial Arboretum, Alrewas